Source movement

Live by five principles that will create
world peace in our lifetime

integrity
responsibility
gratitude
service
community

by Jo Englesson

Jo Englesson.
    Source Movement by Jo Englesson.
    ISBN-13: 978-1-4951-3498-2 (Paperback)

© 2014 Jo Englesson

Publisher: Gratitude Training LLC
        501 Lake Ave
        Lake Worth, FL 33460
        www.gratitudetraining.com

Editor: Kyara Lomer-Camarena
Cover Design: Kwak & Casandra Tanenbaum

dedicated to
my wife
Arian Englesson
and our son
Sixten Alexander Englesson

"Your state of being creates
the world around you."

expressions of
gratitude

i would like to express my gratitude to the people who made this book a possibility and a reality.

To my beautiful wife, Arian, for being the fertile soil where my creativity can flourish and be shared with the world. Your endless love and the sacred space you continuously invite me in to share have grounded me and allowed me to fully express my source-ness in this lifetime and on this planet. I honor and respect you and thank you from the bottom of my heart. You have my heart. I also thank you for the gift of our loved son, our hero, Sixten Alexander Englesson.

To my parents, Marilène and Staffan, and to my big brothers, Johan and Michael, thank you for always showing me that anything is possible and for holding me high. Your unconditional love and willingness to stay open during all my life's trials and tribulations have had me find my own on my own time. Because of you, I always feel safe, and I know that no matter what happens in life, you are always there to welcome me home.

To Francine, my best friend and partner in transformation, because of the stand you are for humanity and the stand you have been for me, there is no doubt in my mind that together we will create world peace in our lifetime. Your three beautiful boys will grow up in a world of unconditional love because you say so. Thank you for your dedication and your loyalty.

To Gary Grant, my coach and teacher, thank you for believing in me and inspiring me to reach for the stars. I am so grateful you kept telling me that I could write a book, and not only that, but you had me do it in 30 days! I cherish our coaching calls every Tuesday and I know that because of you, the world gets to see all of me.

To my spiritual teachers, Ray Blanchard and Bettie Spruill, who believed in me and were willing to do what it takes to support me to start the Gratitude Training in Florida. Thank you for teaching me what it takes to be successful and for holding context for extraordinary results. You are both in my heart, and I am honored to have you in my life.

It is with a deep sense of gratitude that I thank all the members of the Gratitude Community, a community of emerged leaders who are standing as Source for a transformed world NOW! You have all shown me what is possible when a community lives by the principles presented in this book. You inspire me to keep going. You are Source Movement. A special thank you to Chris DeSanti, Kathy Benson and Barry Warren for your passion for the work we do and for lighting the way many times.

I want to thank Kyara Lomer-Camarena for her commitment and expertise as my editor, Casandra Tanenbaum and Kwak for designing a fierce book cover.

table of contents

preface

i have had a book wanting to emerge from within for a while, but I never found the time or, I should say, the courage to actually sit down and write it. So many questions arose every time I attempted: What if it is not as good as I want it to be? What if I am a bad writer? What if people think I am crazy? Who am I to think that I can do something like this? Who's going to want to read it? I can go on, but let me spare you the drama.

One day, after continuously trying to inspire me to write, my life coach (if you don't have one, get one!), had me declare to write a book in 30 days. I thought he was crazy, but being a little nuts myself, I excitedly accepted the challenge. Keep in mind that he wanted me to accomplish this while handling explosive growth in my new company, nurturing a loving relationship, and staying on target with all my other personal and spiritual goals.

I had no idea that it was possible for me to write a book in 30 days. I did not even have a clear topic yet. Nonetheless, I scheduled one hour every morning, three days a week to write. I decided I would sit down and write during this hour regardless if I felt inspired. I made sure I physically sat in front of the

computer with a blank page in front of me, even if I couldn't
write a word.

It was magic. Once I sat down on that first day, words started
flowing from me. I have had a passion to support people to
awaken for so long, and I didn't even realize how much I had
to say. I let go of all my worries about how, when, and what I
should write, and just let it come out.

On the days I had my writing time scheduled, I was always
amazed at how it all flowed once I took the "position" as a
writer. Even up to the last minute before I would sit down to
write, I doubted I had anything to say that day. Yet, without fail,
something would always come. Sometimes, I would sit down and
read what I had written the previous days, and that would jog my
inspiration. I was being a writer. It was no longer about what I
should do; it was about assuming the role and habits of a writer
that supported me in completing the first draft in 30 days.

The title, Source Movement, came to me on March 8, 2013.
I attended a seminar the night before, and I was on my way to
a retreat weekend with one of our leadership teams. I thought
about how my life was so drastically different, or transformed,
from just six years prior. I realized the biggest contribution to
my grateful, abundant, and joyous life was the simple fact that I
started to believe that I create my reality, that I am responsible
for all my results in my life and that I am Source for it all. Not
only that, I was also becoming grateful for everything, and that
catapulted me into an abundant world.

I wanted to share my experience and successes with the world
so everyone would have a choice to wake up every day excited
and ready to live a life of no regrets. I thought about the main

principles by which I had lived to generate my results, and they were clear as day: Integrity, Responsibility, Gratitude, Service, and Community. I felt we were experiencing mass awakening on the planet, and I wanted to put a name to it: Source Movement. I decided to call it a movement because awakening does not happen by itself. Most of the time, others guide us; some aware they are teaching us, and some are not. Once we become aware and then make a choice to be the change for others to awaken, we are part of a movement. Simply put, we are generating an abundance of awakening events; we become the generators—the Source —of a movement.

introduction

What you are about to read in this book can change your life forever—if you choose for it to do so. You are the one reading and listening to the information. You will interpret it how you want to interpret it. In fact, in some aspect, you are actually writing it. We will get to that later, but for now, my invitation is that you intend for this book to transform your life and forever alter how you experience yourself in your life, your family, your community and in the world. I know this is a bold way to begin a book, but why would we intend anything else? Why would we (you and I) write a book that will just change some aspects of our lives or barely educate us in some concepts and distinctions? Why would you want to read a book that merely takes what you have and makes it a little better and a little different? Why not declare big and say, "This book will transform my life!"

Throughout the book, you will sometimes see me write we, as in, "We are writing this book" or "We invite you to . . ." rather then using I. This is because I believe the only way creation can really occur is together as one. We stands for I, you, us, anyone and everyone. So if creation occurs from the all—from everyone as a whole and not solely from the individual—then that would mean painters do not paint their paintings alone, composers do not compose music by themselves, and writers do not single-handedly write their books. What I am getting at is that creation is drawn out and inspired by the collective consciousness of the all—painted, composed or written by the world's desire to appreciate it (or criticize it!). I am not implying that the artists do not have any responsibility in the creation process. They do! They are the ones who actually put the brush to the canvas, fingers on the piano or pen to the paper. Furthermore, they are also fully responsible for what is being created.

Am I confusing you yet? Good. For now, let's see if I can put it in simple terms: We are all energetic beings. Energetically we are vibrating at different frequencies. When I am sad and depressed, my vibration is on a lower frequency, and when I am joyous and loving, I am vibrating at a higher frequency. Are you with me so far? Let's take it further. If you are at a low frequency, the only things available to you are low-frequency people, places, events, and manifestations. On the other hand, if you are standing in joy and love, vibrating high, you will attract high-vibration people, places, events and manifestations. Now the question is: Who can change your vibration? YOU!!! Can you now see how this makes us all responsible for everything within and outside of us? We are the ones choosing the frequency. You will hear me refer to this frequency as vibration, environment, or context throughout the book and how it is generated by our stories, beliefs and conversations we have about others, the world and ourselves.

"Everything is energy, and that's all there is to it. Match the frequency of the reality you want, and you cannot help but get that reality. It can be no other way. This is not philosophy. This is physics."

—ALBERT EINSTEIN

So let's go back and look at the example of an artist creating a painting. The artist will create within the frequency that they are. Because the beliefs of the artist—or the stories and conversations they have about themselves or the world—generate the frequency, the art will reflect that. Moreover, the frequency or vibration of the artist will attract other similar vibrations, and together what will manifest is a painting created within that specific vibration, appreciated and criticized by people of the same vibration. This is how the artist is responsible for the end result, not just because he painted it by himself, but because he simply attracted a certain environment, or context, for the painting to manifest. Simultaneously, this is also how the collective consciousness of that specific frequency creates the context where the art is created. In general terms, we can put it this way: All our results are generated from a specific context (or environment). Our beliefs, both conscious and unconscious, create this context. Others with similar context or beliefs to yours can easily join in, and together, you end up co-creating what you see around you—your results.

So if I am a painter and I don't think I am good enough to be a painter, it will be reflected in my art and my success as an artist. In that case, I am simply not an environment for "good art." If I am a writer and I have a thought that no one will read my book, chances are they won't! So, when I say that we are writing this book and that it will transform your life, it is because I believe that I am good enough to have that happen, and if you picked up this book to read it, you are aligned with that conversation and tuned into that frequency. Simply put, you are good enough to write a book, and why not this one?

I want you to know that everything in this book (as in life) is completely made up. I am making that up, too. You get to choose what you want to believe. I am simply sharing my experience, my views, and my own beliefs. I have found, over time, beliefs and stories that work for me. I have chosen beliefs about the world and myself that create abundance and success in my life. I have chosen to hold them as true for me. This is what I want to share with you. I will make no attempt to back up my view or supply endless research to prove my point. There will be no reason for me to defend or claim that what I am sharing in this book is the Truth. It is not. Or is it? You decide. What I will do, however, is make some majorly bold declarations, statements and assumptions. Because I can. I am not channeling any other dimensions (at least not yet!). I am simply collecting my thoughts and what I have learned, read and been taught over the years and putting them on paper as my truth. I invite you to try it on. Try on the concepts and if you choose to hold it as Truth with a capital T because you find that it works for you in your life, so be it. If you choose to discard it because it does not align with what you hold as truth, so be it. If you want access to the backup or research that could be behind this book, don't come to me for it. Find the answers for yourself. There is nothing more powerful than doing your own questioning and searching, whether it is from within or outside of you. Your answers will be true for you. It is my intention that this book will evoke the right questions for you, and therefore, open a new possibility.

I am a guru, and so are you. We all are. On the purest level, we are anything and everything. We are infinite beings with full potential. We are all masters, gurus, and virtuosos. We all have incredible gifts and functions to be expressed in our lifetime. If we are not expressing those yet, it is because of two reasons: either we have not yet discovered our true calling, our "gift," or we have an unaligned conversation about expressing and living it. For most people, on the deepest level, these unaligned conversations are "I am not good enough," "Who am I to think I can do it?" or "I am not worthy of it." In this book, we will explore these and other conversations we have and how they generate our results and our environment. We will see how changing these unaligned conversations to new conversations that support us in generating what we say we want will bring abundance in all areas of our life.

A quick note here: We will use the word conversation often in this book. We use it to describe all the things we tell ourselves about the world, others, and ourselves. It describes the beliefs and stories we have made up. If I tell myself that I can't do something or that I don't deserve love or that I am a bad writer, my conversation about myself is most likely on the deepest level that I am not good enough.

unaligned conversations

So what do I mean when I say that it is our unaligned conversations that stop us from expressing our gifts and functions? I am simply saying that on some deep level, you have a belief about yourself that is not in alignment with who you authentically are or say you want to be. An unaligned conversation would be you wanting to become a doctor and at the same time you having a belief from childhood that you are too stupid to be a doctor. Until the deeper belief or conversation is shifted to align with what you want, you will not create the result you want. What you will do, however, is quit medical school, blame your bad grades on your teacher, party too much, or whatever else to be right about the fact that you, on some level, believe you are too stupid to be a doctor. It's powerful what we do! We are masters at creating the results that are in alignment with the beliefs we have and the conversations we are. Too bad these are not always the results we want!

What if we could be as masterful at shifting the beliefs into something that will actually align with what we really want, rather then creating results that align with our conversations about our smallness? What would be possible then? We spend energy proving our beliefs right rather than spending energy on shifting the belief so we can have the results we really want. We are totally focusing our energy on the wrong thing!

your parrot

This notion of conversations, beliefs, and stories is so important that I want to give you an illustration that can support you as you read on. Imagine there is a parrot caged inside your head from the moment you were born. It loves to learn words and sentences from everyone and everything, and tends to constantly repeat everything for you to hear. Your parrot—feel free to name it—tells you things, good and bad.

For instance, if you were told in school you had a learning disability and would never be able to learn properly, your parrot gladly repeated that to you until you believed it. Or maybe your dad was disrespectful to your mom, and your parrot told you men are disrespectful, and now you can't seem to keep a relationship because of it.

Your parrot can also tell you things that support you in life. For instance, say you were brought up in a financially abundant family who told you it is easy to make money. In this case, your parrot may repeat that, and now you find it easy to make money and create abundance. Some of the things our parrots say we can hear loud and clear; they are conscious to us. Other things said are more in the background, and we may not really hear them, even though they still shape the way we live our lives. These stories our parrots tell us are unconscious; they are there, and they affect us, but we are not aware of them, and we can't hear them.

It is important to understand how impressionable your parrot is, especially when you are a child. It picks up everything and repeats it back to you. The loudest stories and conversations your parrot has are usually the ones that don't serve you so well in life. The parrot loves these stories and has learned to love drama over the years. This is because the world we live in today promotes this. But there is hope! At its core, your parrot is neutral and can still learn; it still picks up conversations and stories all the time. All you have to do is train it! Train it to say something different—to tell you things that will support you, stories and conversations that will support your vision and your dreams. If we were ego-less people, we may argue that we would not even need the parrot to tell us anything, but let's face it; we are not! So our best bet is to use our awesome parrot to create world peace with us.

When we refer to stories and conversations, you can imagine that these are the things your parrot tells you about you, others and the world. Your parrot is having conversations with you that you have entertained for decades. These conversations have now become your beliefs out of which you live your life. I say, let's teach our parrots who's the boss here!

In order to know what our stories and conversations are, we have to become aware of them—become aware of what we are thinking and how it generates everything in our reality. This book will assist you not only in becoming aware but will also will give you tools and principles to live by to stay present so you can continuously align your gifts with your vision for the world.

awakening our planet

We are at a very interesting time in history with an endless wave of people awakening to who they authentically are. People are awakening to something new, something beyond themselves. Many people are starting to believe they actually are divine and the creator of their own reality. Some are allowing God in for the first time; some are altering their belief about God from previously learned belief systems to a newfound relationship with God.

When I say God, I am not talking about a man with a beard in the sky; I am referring to that greater part of us that forms our oneness and creates our reality. In this book, we will refer to that as *SOURCE*. My invitation is that you allow whatever word you use—God, Allah, Shiva, Love, Peace—to be synonymous with Source. We will explore something I call "Source Movement" and the principles of living a life in alignment with your vision for the world, fully expressing your talents and living on purpose. We will explore how we will have world peace in our lifetime simply by living by these principles: Integrity, Responsibility, Gratitude, Service, and Community. Are you up for that?

Source Movement is individuals and communities coming together for the purpose of awakening the planet with the end goal of generating world peace in our lifetime. We are currently in the middle of Source Movement. Since it is occurring over time, from a linear timeline perspective, we may not realize we are actually in one of the most exciting times of our history. We are awakening to our purpose, and as Eckhart Tolle would say, to a New Earth. A thousand years from now, this time will be merely a dot on a timeline, which is why we may not always see what really is happening while in the middle of it. Maybe people will spend endless time in the future writing about us and about what occurred. Maybe they will analyze it, summarize it, and put a name to it. We will support them and get aware and write about it now while we are in it. We will give it a name.

We call it Source Movement. We use the word Source because we are all the point of origin, the creator, of the movement. We call it a movement because we are generating an abundance of events, a movement of awakening. Standing at the helm of

Source Movement, we can use our awareness to be the generators, the Source of the movement. At the core of this movement, we accept that we are Source for everything, we take responsibility to create peace in our lifetime, and we have it happen because we say so.

If this is something you can align with, I ask that you join this movement and begin to embody these five principles in your life. If this sounds like too much to take on or too hard to get behind, please read on anyway. This book will support you to find peace for you as an individual, as well, which in turn has you be Source for world peace by default.

I welcome you to Source Movement.

chapter two

what is source?

hat is Source? This is a very BIG question. It is similar to asking, "What is God?" or "What is the meaning of life?" If you look up the word "source" in a dictionary, there are several different meanings. We will look at the following three translations from Merriam-Webster.com: a generative force-CAUSE, a point of origin-BEGINNING and one that initiates-AUTHOR. For those who believe in God, Allah or Shiva, or anyone else, isn't that what most of them are? A causal energy, a point of origin, who authors (creates) everything?

When you create something in this physical world, wouldn't you say there is a piece of you in it? When you create a child, isn't there a part of you in that child? Yet, that child will still have free will to create by herself in this world. That is how we will look at Source —an all-encompassing energy that creates

11

everything as itself without the need to control it or judge its fate. Source's only desire, if energy can have desire, is to see its creations, namely us, express our source-ness on this planet. So how do we do that? How do we express our source-ness?

We are creative beings, always creating something. The question is, are we creating what we want, or are we left with results and drama that we don't want? The first step in accepting the idea that we are Source is to accept the notion that we are actually creating both what we want and the stuff we don't want. We are always standing as Source for something. We constantly generate what we see in our world. Our energy or vibration is always the cause of our reality and our results. We constantly author things into our life. So the question is not: How do I stand as Source? The question really is: How do I stand as Source for what I want? How do I stand as Source for love and peace?

So let's break this down a little bit. I am not asking that you believe everything that is presented in this book. Some concepts may not work for you and your beliefs at this time, and I honor that. My invitation is that you, if only for a moment, suspend your disbelief and "try it on." At the end of the book, you can drop everything you have read and go back to your original beliefs. Deal?

As a being in the Source Movement, you are standing as the creator (author) of your reality. You are responsible for EVERY-THING. You generate ALL the results you have in your life—the divorce, the promotion, the loss of a loved one, the dream house, etc. The concept of "I create EVERYTHING" can be challenging for some of us. Over the years, we have adapted many different beliefs of God, our results, our relationships, our life, and ourselves. Most of us have operated from a place of "none of this is my fault"—from a place of being a victim to our reality, to our results and to other people. This has given us some benefits (otherwise we wouldn't do it!). One of the benefits is that we don't have to be responsible for the "bad" stuff that shows up in our life.

What is happening today in the world is many people are awakening to a different belief, a different conversation. They are starting to accept ancient concepts and spiritual teachings about actually being the author of it all; being the creator of their world. That is how we will look at it. You are the creator and the causal factor in everything that occurs in this world. As long as there is war in the world, you are war-ing somewhere in your existence. As long as there are people who steal from others, you are stealing somewhere in your life (maybe you are stealing time from people by always being late). As long as children are dying from hunger, you are starving somewhere in your life (maybe you do not have the abundance of love that you desire). It does not always look the way we think it would look. It is not a "tit for tat" concept. It is simply a place to stand as Source, a place of power to be able to understand that you can actually be the catalyst for change, the Source for something else to show up.

Many people don't want to take the responsibility for the bad things in the world. I say, why not? If I do, then I can easily shift the things in my life and make a bigger difference as a whole. Don't you agree that if I stop being selfish and fighting in my relationship, someone else will be positively affected by it? I will even go as far as to say that on an energetic level, me changing WILL change others with whom I have not even come in contact. That is what living as Source will do. What a fun game to play!

the human X game

If I was my higher self or my spirit self, or Source, and I chose to have a human experience, here is how I would set it up. I will illustrate this in very simple board-game-like terms by creating a metaphor to attempt to explain why we are here. Let's have some fun with this:

We will call my spirit self "Jossan" [pronounced yo-ssan]. So one day, Jossan was hanging out in the world we will call the Other Dimension with all the other spirits and nonphysical beings. Because they are all in nonphysical form, it can get a little confusing in the Other Dimension; sometimes they don't really know who they are. Most of the time, they are just part of everyone else and have no physical distinction to separate from each other. Life is grand here, as there is not much to worry about; there is nothing to do, to figure out, and to feel or be. Once in a while, some of the spirits decide to sit down and play a game called "HumanX"—they do this because it is the best game out there. This game brings ups and downs, excitement and contrast, and it is fun to play. Many of them play this game over and over again because they love it!

Here is how the game works: Each player picks a Token to play with called a Human. They then draw a Contract Card that will be attached to the Human. The card has some set parameters for life experiences and personality qualities of their Human. They will then roll the dice, and instantaneously their Human is born and alive in the world we will call HumanX, or the Human Experience. In this moment, the control is given to the Human, even though the Human is actually a small part of all of them. But here is the catch: The moment the Human is placed in HumanX, he or she does not remember any of this. This is where the fun begins. The way you win this game is simply by having your Token, your Human, "get" that they are more then just human; get that this is just a game and that there is a bigger part of us as one; get that we are all one.

So in my case, Jossan decided to play this game. She chose a Human and a Contract Card that manifested as me, Jo Englesson, being born in Sweden with two older brothers waiting for her and parents who loved her. The game was on! When I imagine Jossan sitting up there watching me "play" the game of life and going over all that has occurred thus far, it makes me laugh! Wow! In the game, the more aware your Human is, the more power the spirit will have to create within the game. Also, the Human is given an EGO. The EGO is another part created from Jossan, from the spirit, from the all. The EGOs function is to make sure the Humans do not understand that they are playing a game, to make sure that the Humans do not awaken to who they really are. This is also a fun part of the game. The EGO will generate worlds and events that will have the Humans certain they are not the ones creating everything, that they are not Source.

For instance, imagine you are walking down the street and think of a penny. Then suddenly there is a penny on the sidewalk right in front of you. You think, "Wow, how powerful I am; I manifested a penny right in front of me." We may look at it as a sign of our power and us being the creator. Then you bend down to pick it up, and next to it is a candy wrapper, a piece of trash lying on this beautiful street in your town and you think, "Why do people just throw their trash all over the place?" And you get disappointed at "the world." Well, here is the catch: You placed the wrapper there, too. Your ego-self, which is committed to have you not get that you create everything, put the wrapper there. That is why the game is so fun to play. The ego is brilliant, as brilliant as your spirit self. Once you become aware of this, you can start to have fun with it. What a great journey!

It took me a while to realize I was just a game piece on a game board, but now that I know, it is so much more fun to be in this existence. At the same time, I am aware that I am making all this up, so who really knows? I do know this, though: I am having a grand time viewing my existence from this conversation, from having this story about it. Try it on. Teach your parrot something new!

So what is Source? It is the oneness and the all-encompassing consciousness and energy of everything. It is the causal energy that creates our existence. At the heart of the Source Movement is a declaration that everyone awakens to who they authentically are and, as a result, becomes an expression of peace in the world. This is what will have each of us individually be the cause of peace. This is why we are writing this book—to get that we all matter, that we are a gift and a contribution to life and are an integral Source for world peace.

chapter three

vision

et's start by taking a look at why we bother reading about awakening, authorship, source, responsibility, and the endless self-help books that line the shelves at our bookstores. What are we really looking for? Why do we attend seminars, workshops and classes, and converse endlessly about why we are here? Or maybe you have not done any of that, but you have thought about it, haven't you? You've thought, "What is really the point? How can I be happier? How can I enhance my relationships? How can I make more money? How can I be a better parent?" Well, there are a lot of answers out there, and many of them will have you get closer to what you want.

So the first question is: What do you want? Have you spent any time trying to answer that question? For example, a wife complains that her husband is lazy because he doesn't help around the house or doesn't take her out on dates. But has she stepped back and thought about what she wants in a relationship? What is her vision of a perfect relationship? Chances are she never thought of that. She had been so busy thinking about all the things that were wrong and all the things she did not want that there was no time to get clear on what she really wanted. From that place, there is no possibility to create anything. It is a dead space. Many of us live our lives from that dead space.

Without a clear vision of what we want in our life, in our community, and in the world, it is difficult and almost impossible to meet the goals and generate the results we really want. Therefore, the first invitation is to get clear on your vision. Your vision is the ultimate wish and dream you have about your life and for the world. Your vision should make your heart sing. I want to draw a quick distinction here between vision and goals. Goals are more like milestones and benchmarks toward your greater vision. For instance, if your vision is to be in integrity, your goals on the way toward that vision could be to pay your bills on time. Many people tend to focus only on their goals, such as winning a game or increasing their salary. If we don't have a clear vision behind our goals, something that has us understand why it is important to win the game or what an increased salary would mean in the bigger picture, most of the time we will not be as successful in accomplishing them. Your vision for the world is how you want the world to be. So what is your vision? What is your vision for your life, for your family, for the world? What do you really want?

A great start to get clear is to ask yourself, "If I could not fail, what would I go for?" Many times, we are scared to dream and set goals toward our dreams because we don't believe it is possible, and we are afraid to fail. We are afraid to be disappointed. I say dare to dream! Make your vision big!

Here is an exercise that may support you in creating or getting clear on your vision. You may want to put a muzzle on your parrot during this exercise. Write down or think about your vision for each of the areas listed below. Think of it this way: If you had a magic wand and you could have it exactly the way you wanted it, what would you want in each specific area? Get specific and juicy. Go for it!

- ⊃ Health/Wellness/Personal Growth/Spirituality
- ⊃ Financial Abundance—Includes Work/Career/ Professional Goals
- ⊃ Relationships
  - Romantic
  - Immediate/Extended Family
  - Friends
- ⊃ Community
- ⊃ The World

Was it hard to come up with a vision for some of the areas? Which ones? We invite you to work some more on these if you see that it will support you in getting clear. Notice if you kept thinking about what you don't want. If you did, you may just have been listening to the programming of your parrot. The parrot is very good at reiterating what we don't want. Give it another try! Be aware of changing the "don't wants" to what you do want. For instance, shift "I don't want to be fat" to "I want to be healthy" or "I don't want to work 9 to 5" to "I want a job that gives me freedom to set my own hours."

Once you are clear on your vision, you are immediately standing at a new point of possibility. From this place, you can start declaring actions, goals, ways of being and emotions that will forward you toward that vision. For instance, if my vision for my family is to live on a farm with horses and have my kids in private school, I can now begin to take some action toward that or change a way of being that will work better toward having that or work on my beliefs and emotions around what I deserve for myself—or all of the above! If, on the other hand, I stay in a place of complaining about my kids' current school and expressing sadness about not having horses, etc., chances are this is where I will stay.

The neat thing about having a vision that drives you is this: You can use it to make things happen! I run a transformational training and leadership program called Gratitude Training out of West Palm Beach, Florida, and one of the principles of leadership we stand by is: My vision, commitments, and promises are what dictates my way of being and my actions, not my judgments, circumstances or feelings. I want to tell you a story that illuminates the truth behind this statement for me.

the don warms story

At age 36, my marriage was failing, my career was dwindling, and I had a pending foreclosure. So I decided to move to Florida and was excited to start anew. The only problem was that all my circumstances moved with me. My now-ex-wife told me about a life-altering training she had heard about and suggested I check it out, so I enrolled. I did not know then that this was going to be the first pivotal moment in my life and in my own personal awakening. I completed the three-part training in a four-month period. While in the third part, the second life-changing event occurred.

I was at an airport in New York, and I was rushing toward the gate to catch my flight. I accidentally ran into an older gentleman, about 80 years old, and we both nearly fell to the ground. I immediately started bracing myself, as I was certain this man would give me a lecture and tell me what a horrible person I was. But I was wrong. Instead, the man, whose name was Don Warms, turned to me and hugged me and said, "No worries, I bet you do this all the time!" Then he laughed and turned to me with a grandfatherly look just before he took his granddaughter by the hand and walked away. I was standing there watching him leave, and I suddenly felt an intense feeling of gratitude for life and people. I wanted to give him something in return, a token of my appreciation. I realized how important it is that we act from love and that we honor and appreciate each other. No matter what.

I boarded the plane, still in awe over the "moment of gratitude" that just occurred. I was reflecting on my whole life as I sat in my seat looking out over the beautiful clouds beneath me, and I realized, "I am flying." Something awakened in me. I felt a sense of calm and a sense of deep gratitude. I wanted to share this with the world. A vision and a deeper sense of purpose were emerging. I started thinking; "What if we had something we could give each other in that moment of appreciation and gratitude, a token of appreciation? A coin! I got it! I was going to create a coin—a token that simply says, "Thank you for making a difference in my day." I also decided I would put a unique serial number on each coin so it could be tracked online as it travels from person to person. I was going to make a difference in the world!

It turned out Don Warms was on my flight, and I had a chance to thank him again, get his contact information and tell him what I was committed to create because of him. That day, TOFA (Token of Appreciation) was born.

A year later, to the date, I had 1,000 tokens manufactured and numbered, and I launched the tracking website, TOFA.us. That day, I drove to Don Warms' house unannounced to give him token No. 1 and thank him for making a difference in my LIFE. On this day, I started something I call "The Giving Year." I made a commitment to give away one token every day for 365 days and document every "Token Moment" on YouTube. I had no idea what this one-year journey would do for me and for the people I encountered. In fact, some days were difficult days, where I was simply in my "stuff" and was not "feeling it." These days I learned some of the most valuable lessons. I was choosing from committed action and vision rather than choosing from how I was feeling. Once I went out in the world, generating a moment to be grateful for, I realized how important it is for us to stand in gratitude and appreciation and committed action to create amazing results in our lives.

Toward the end of the Giving Year, I started seeing amazing changes in my personal life, both financially and emotionally. I manifested the house I wanted to live in. I say "manifest" because I was becoming more and more aware of what I was creating, and I realized it was not chance that threw all these amazing opportunities my way. I was opening a space for it by standing in gratitude and appreciation. I created the relationships I wanted. Money was beginning to flow. And most importantly, joy and peace were now a way of life, a state of mind, rather than something outside of me to strive for.

This is just one of the hundreds of amazing stories from this year: About six months into the Giving Year, I was renting a room at a friends house and I had just landed a great marketing job in Boca Raton, Florida. I was ready to find my own place to live, something I had desired ever since my divorce a year earlier. I began to search for places online and after a few days I found my dream house within my spending limit. I had just started my new job and was not in a financial position to act yet. I wanted to move in about two months later so I didn't bother to call about it. I did, however, keep browsing to the link online every day and look at the pictures and dream about living there. About two weeks after first finding it, I decided to go to a drum circle. I had never been to this place before, and I didn't know anyone there. There were about 100 people there, and I found a spot next to a drummer named David. After a while, we began to chat, and he told me he was a Realtor and that he also owned a couple properties. I told him what I was looking for by describing the dream house I had been looking at online for the past two weeks. David looked at me and said, "That sounds like one of my houses." With the help of my iPhone, I pulled up the house I wanted, and David was dumbfounded. It was one of his houses! Then he says, "We have a tenant living there that is not ready to move out for two months." Unbelievable! Two months later, I moved in to my new house!

The Giving Year is a perfect example of standing in a vision and acting from commitment rather than being a victim to the circumstances of life. Circumstances are always going to be there, trust me! Vision and commitment will not erase your circumstances, but they will alter the relationship you have with them. Think about it: We all know people who have very little money, and somehow they always create enough to do anything they want. We also know people who have a lot of money but seem to still struggle financially. It is not the amount of money that gives us abundance; it is simply the relationship and the conversations we have about money. What does our parrot say about money? When we are willing to change some of the beliefs and stories we have about what we hold as circumstances, we start altering how they affect us, and we can ultimately alter our results. So how do we do that? We get clear on a really juicy vision and get committed to it. Vision is the key to put you on the path of living a purposeful life in joy and gratitude. So if you did not do the vision exercise presented earlier in this chapter, do it now. It will make a huge difference in how the rest of your life turns out.

Vision + Committed Action + Community (Team)
= Extraordinary Results

                                        – Gratitude Training LLC

five principles

In the introduction, we spoke about Source Movement and the principles for living a life in alignment with our vision for the world. Now that we have explored what Source means and the importance of vision, it is time to dive into the five principles—Integrity, Responsibility, Gratitude, Service, and Community.

Before we begin, let's explore what a principle is. Here are two definitions of the word principle from Oxford Dictionaries:

1. A fundamental truth or proposition that serves as the foundation for a system of belief or behavior or for a chain of reasoning.
2. A rule or belief governing one's personal behavior.

You choose how to see the principles in this book—as a guide, rules, or truths to live by, or you can simply see them as a set of recommendations that could enhance your life. You may already have principles in place that are working well in creating what you want. These five principles are not to replace or discard any other principles by which you live. Ultimately you will choose *your* principles. I invite you to open a space for these five principles in your life. They work. I personally have made a conscious choice to live by them, and as a result, my life is extraordinary, and I see peace happening in our lifetime.

We could say that these five principles will have you live as Source, but the real question is: Source for what? If we are not specific about what we want to create in our lives, our communities and the world, we are simply just living as Source for something else, most likely Source for the limiting beliefs and conversations that run us. Is that really what we want to generate in the world? Do we really want our "not good enough" conversations to be the context in which our children grow up? Do we want our fears and lack of trust to set the environment for our lives and our future? Do we want control and fear of rejection to run our relationships? Do we want our judgments, frustrations, and anger to make the decisions in warfare?

There is no Source Movement without the awareness that we are the creator of everything and that we generate the world we see. These principles are simply a guide, a stand, a set of rules that will support us in generating that awareness so together we can create peace and love everywhere. I say *together* because once we are aware that we are the sole creator of everything, we will also see that we are all one. There is no separation.

Integrity, Responsibility, Gratitude, Service, and Community are the titles of the Source Movement principles. I say titles because without delving into the meaning of them as a distinction of the Source Movement, the words can be interpreted in thousands of ways. Also, "community" by itself as a word is not a principle by definition. However, if I were to say, "my principle is to work as a community to change the world," that could create a belief that would have me change my behavior, a principle by which to live.

I'm going to ask you to try something on, even if only for the time you are reading the rest of this book. I want you to believe that living by these five principles directly relates to living a life fully expressed and on purpose, a life with you as the generator, a life where you create all the results you want, a life of joy and peace. Be willing to embody the notions, the distinctions, and the tools. If you do, I promise you will see a major shift in your life, and we all will begin to see a shift on this planet. Sound bold? Good. If a little boldness can transform the planet; let's welcome it!

I chose Integrity, Responsibility, Gratitude, Service, and Community as principles from having experienced them in my life. I have not read a bunch of books about them, nor have I researched them in any extent. Through both spiritual and non-spiritual life experiences, encounters with teachers I've met, and transformational trainings, I personally had life experiences with each principle—experiences that have allowed me to embody these distinctions in my life. Some of the experiences were through difficult life events, such as divorce, alcoholism and death, and some were simply by being at the right place at the right time.

Looking back, I am now clear that I created all the events and that *being at the right place at the right time* is just me being

aligned with what I want, my vision. During most of these learning experiences, I was not conscious to the lessons and the real
"whys" of what was happening. But in 2007, I attended a transformational training that hit me over the head with a two-by-
four. Attending this workshop was by far the most powerful
experience of awakening I had up until that time in my life. I
became aware of everything that stopped me, learned the tools
to shift my life and understood that I am responsible for everything. I realized how I was living my life from circumstance and
judgments rather than from possibility and acceptance. I got
what being "in integrity" really meant. It was during the third
part of this training, a three-month leadership program, when I
ran into Don Warms who inspired me to create TOFA. I understood what a vision-driven life was when I spent a year giving out
tokens during the Giving Year. I got what being in service meant
as I volunteered endlessly for organizations that were a commitment to transform people's lives and, in doing so, this planet.
I understood what community really was, when I started my
first transformational training center, Gratitude Training LLC,
and, as a result, the Gratitude Community. Today, the Gratitude
Trainings are changing lives all over the world, and it is my commitment that everyone attends. I am certain it is the fastest way
to world peace. If you know of a faster way, let me know, and I
will follow!

The next chapter is about how our "conversations" produce
everything in our life. It is an important concept and the core of
Source Movement's principles. The following five chapters outline the principles.

At the end of each chapter, there will be some powerful

questions for you to answer; this is an opportunity for self-reflection. There also will be a Call to Action section in which we outline some steps you can take to test-drive the concepts and each principle in your life.

Although the following chapters somewhat build on each other, it is not necessary to read them in order. In fact, if you feel stuck or lost in one of the chapters, I encourage you to skip and read ahead. Something may open up later that will help you go back and read from a new perspective.

chapter five

our conversations

et's take a look at how our stories and conversations really produce our results and that there is a direct link between them and what we create. When I say that we all have conversations that produce every single result in our life, on some level I am saying that we are a "walking conversation." I want you to think of yourself as a conversation. In simple terms: you are what you think. I am using the word conversation to illustrate the following:

- What we say about ourselves, others and the world
- Our beliefs about ourselves, others and the world
- Our thoughts
- Our stories we have made up about everything

For instance, if I am overweight and can't seem to lose weight, most likely, I have a belief, or a story, that is deep within me about being fat, about weight, or about self-worth—a *conversa-tion* that aligns my actions and my results with "being fat." As long as I have this internal conversation (belief) about it, it does not matter how many times I successfully lose weight because I will always gain it back. On the other hand, if I can become aware of what the conversation is, I can begin to shift the belief so that new results can be created.

fact versus story

We all have beliefs and conversations about ourselves. We all make up stories about everything. If we can let go of the notion that our stories and beliefs are "true" or "right," then we can start making up some better stories that will make us feel better and create what we want. Again, remember the parrot. If we make it all up, why not make it up great? Teach your parrot what to tell you.

The key to shift our conversations about things—to change what the parrot tells us—is to be able to distinguish *facts* from *the story we have about the fact*. If you can master this, you will be free. You will be able to decide how you see and interpret every event in your life. This concept can be difficult to grasp because we are human after all, and there are some stories we hold as facts no matter what.

For instance, if I say, "The cup is on the table," and it can be verified that it is, we can all agree that it is a fact. If someone hit your car, the fact is "someone hit your car." So what story or conversation could we make up about your car being hit? Let's explore a few: "I am a bad driver." "The person who hit me is a jerk." "He was not paying attention." "If he hadn't been on the phone, he would not have hit me." "My life is over; I can't afford to fix my car." We could go on forever. Some of these may be facts. My invitation is to become aware of all the stories you make up around an event, specifically the ones that may not serve you.

For instance, let's say you make up that you are a bad driver, and you believe that is true. Chances are that this conversation about yourself—"I am a bad driver"—will keep generating "bad driver" experiences in your life. It may also add to a deeper conversation you may have about yourself that says, "I am not good at anything" or "I am not enough." You are simply collecting more and more evidence to be right about something you hold as true. Could it be true that you are a bad driver? Sure. But here is the key: If you work on shifting that conversation about yourself, you may have a new platform to create something different that works better in your life. I use the word *may* because we don't know if that is true either! Here is what I do know, though. Shifting the conversation to something that is more fun could have you continue to be a bad driver, if that is the case, but could make you be able to laugh about it and not make it part of WHO you ARE. Ultimately, you have the key. You can make the choice. You create it all!

with awareness comes choice

Unfortunately, many of our stories and conversations we have are unconscious. We are simply not aware they are there, and we act automatically. For instance, some people may not be aware that the main reason they don't have financial abundance is because they have a belief that money is bad or it's hard to make money. Some people are aware of the stories but have chosen at some point to make them so real and so true that they're simply not willing to make a different choice. There is a reason they choose to keep them.

Let's look at an example of this. You can apply it to any of your own stories. Let's say you are a single, straight woman, and you really want a loving, connected relationship with your dream man. At the same time, you have a belief that "men can't be trusted" or "men are scum." You are fully aware you feel this way and entertain many conversations with yourself and others about it. You may even be aware that having that conversation is most likely not going to attract your dream guy. But you keep the conversation anyway. Why? Because it protects your ego! It makes your parrot right! The parrot loves to be right! On some level, this story protects you from fear of rejection, from fear of losing someone you love, from being hurt. The story will push them away before you even begin the relationship. Simply put, you are aware you have the story, and you choose to keep it to protect yourself. The payoff is that you get to be safe. The price may be that you can't fully be in relationship with people.

Look at all your beliefs and ask yourself: Am I keeping this story to be safe? At what cost? What am I missing out on by holding on to my conversation? Is it preventing me from what I really want? Preventing me from my vision? Is it causing others to stay stuck in their stories, too? Is this who I want to be?

This is where the work begins. If you can discover all the conversations and stories you have about everything and get clear on if they work or don't work for you in your life, then you have

begun your journey toward freedom and joy. Once you can identify the conversation that you are, you open up the doors to possibility and to an abundance of new choices. You may wonder
how you can identify the unconscious stories you have, the ones
that you are not even aware of. Keep reading. You will uncover
many of them by reading this book and by applying the five
principles of Source Movement in your life. Once you awaken
to a new way of thinking, a new way of seeing life, most of your
unconscious beliefs and conversations will become conscious.

you are your conversation

Our conversations and stories define how we show up in life. I
believe that we are all one and that the only thing that separates
us and has us show up differently is the stories we have about
ourselves and others. I am not talking about our uniqueness; I
do believe all of us are unique and have different purposes here.
I am simply saying that if we are all one, then I am part of you,
part of God, part of the trees, part of a child and part of a murderer. So let's go a little deeper—actually, a lot deeper.

The next sentence is very bold. *The only difference between
a murderer and myself is a conversation.* Be with that statement
for a little bit. Read it again. It is a very powerful statement. We
are all the same. What shows up and how we act and are, are
just results of what we say about ourselves. Our parrots are just
trained differently. If you can get this, it may open up a space
for forgiveness and compassion for people in your life and for
people in this world. Imagine they just have their parrot telling
them things that have them show up and act the way they do. I

am not letting them off the hook here; we are all responsible for our own awareness and the choices we make. However, based on the level of awareness we are at, we may not all have the same choices available to us. So if how we show up is directly related to our conversations we have and not necessarily who we are, then isn't it possible that I could be the exact same as a murderer and that the only difference between us is a conversation? Without the thoughts, beliefs and stories producing our actions and ways of being, who would we be? Who are we really? How can we have our conversations without them having us?

What if it is absolutely true for some people that the only choice they know to discipline their children is to spank them? What if they are not able to comprehend that there may be another more effective and less painful way while still being in alignment with the principles they have? Would you judge them? Would you tell them they are wrong? What if it is possible for you to be the space for them to see another possibility and to cause them to awaken to a new story? What if you could support them in teaching their parrot some new lines? What if you got that because you still have your parrot on automatic about other things, you are being a cause for their parrot to be on automatic? What if you shifted your conversations and, in turn, theirs would shift, too? What if you could simply love yourself unconditionally? What then?

Let me illustrate this with a personal example. I used to have a story about myself that said: "I never finish anything I start. I will always be just mediocre, never the best or excellent at anything." Through attending a transformational workshop at 36 years of age, I was able to identify this story and ultimately let it go. I was able to make up a new story that would work better for what I was up to in the world. Now the story is: "I am whole, perfect and complete. I deserve to create and complete any projects I choose because I get that I matter and make a difference on this planet."

This new story had me write this book in 30 days (see preface). This new story had me invent and create TOFA (Token of Appreciation). It had me work with superstars of transformation, such as Dr. Ray Blanchard and Ms. Bettie Spruill, to redesign and reinvent the transformational trainings I attended in 2007, and as a result founded Gratitude Training in 2010. Moreover, this new story has me thrive in relationships and in the community. To put it simply, this conversation about myself works, and I am keeping it! What conversation will you choose?

questions for
reflection

1) What are some of the underlying beliefs that hold me back?

   _____

   _____

   _____

2) What are the conversations I have about myself that have me create the results I don't want?

   _____

   _____

   _____

3) Are my stories and beliefs true? Investigate from a neutral place. Get coaching if necessary.

   _____

   _____

   _____

4) Am I willing to be wrong about my conversations in order to create new ones that align better with my vision?

   _____

   _____

   _____

call for
action

➲ Write down all your stories, beliefs and conversations that stop you
  in your life. Take some time and really explore all the things you
  tell yourself about anything. Some examples are, "I never finish
  anything," "It is hard to make money," "If I am open to being
  loved, I get hurt," "I don't deserve this relationship," "I am a loser."
  Write it all down. Then look at all the results you have in your life
  that you are not proud of, and see if you can match them up to any
  of the beliefs you just wrote down. If you want to go really deep,
  list the payoffs you get and the prices you pay for each story you
  have. Payoffs are the goodies you get from keeping the story, and
  prices are what it cost you and others when you have this story.

➲ Make up a new story. Have some fun with this one. Take one
  of the limiting stories you wrote down from the call for action
  above and make up a new story. Then change it to something that
  you think would create a different, more desirable, result. Make
  a commitment to honor this new story as the truth and remind
  yourself often of it. You may want to post it somewhere in your
  house or at work so that you can remind yourself. For instance, if
  you have a conversation about not being romantic, change it to be
  "I am a romantic!" Make an effort to align actions with this new
  conversation, actions that would validate this new story of you.
  Reach out for support and coaching if you need some pointers.
  Notice when you slip into the old story and simply replace it with
  this new one. Make the commitment to be rigorous about this for
  at least seven days. At the end of seven days, write down what you
  learned, and make a choice if you want to keep the new story!

chapter six

first principle: integrity

Source is ALWAYS in integrity, and so am I.
The question is: What conversations
am I in integrity with?

here is a reason Integrity is the first principle. If you understand what integrity is from the perspective we will explore here, you can start shifting your conversations, beliefs, and stories that don't work into those that will support you in creating what you want. Simply put, you can teach your parrot to tell you things that will serve you and support your growth. There is a lot to cover in this chapter. First we will look at three different levels of Integrity. Then we will explore further how our stories and conversations relate to this principle and how we can use the distinction of Integrity as a tool to awaken and become aware of the stories we

41

have. We will also see how *being our word* directly relates to our self-worth.

three levels of integrity

One of my master teachers, Bettie Spruill, speaks of three levels of Integrity. The first level is the level of promise. Do you keep your promises? To create success in the game of life, it is important to establish integrity with yourself, the people with whom you network, and your community. When you consistently break your promises, you start to create an energetic field of not keeping your promises. Since we are all vibrating, energetic beings attracting people similar to us, over time, what we will end up with when we break our word is a group of people around us who break their word, complain, and are controlled by their problems. As a result, we create a community around us who buys into our stories and our circumstances, and we begin to generate results that are not aligned with our vision. Trust me, it's not always easy to keep our promises, but it is key in beginning to generate the life and the results you want. So the first level of Integrity is: *Keep your promises*.

The second level of Integrity is to have a set of principles you won't abandon. What principles do you live by? I live by Source Movement's five principles, and I have chosen to fully and wholeheartedly apply them in my life. Gandhi had a set of principles, and he would not move until he was aligned with his principles. What are the principles you are willing to live in integrity with? The second level of Integrity is: *Live by your principles*.

The third level of Integrity is to honor your word as yourself.

This is honoring who you say you are. Be who you say you are. If you say you are loving, be loving. If you say you are true to your word, be true to your word. If you say you are responsible, be responsible. If you say you are a good parent, be a good parent. Be who you say you are all the time, not only when the circumstances are right. Don't wait for the conditions to be favorable for you to be who you say you are. Be it now. Be it all the time. The third level of Integrity is: *Honor your word as yourself.*

When we break our word, regardless of what level of Integrity we look at, all that is happening is that we are making a *conversation* more important then keeping our word. For instance, if I give my word to be on time to a meeting and I show up late, on some level, I must have listened to a belief I have about myself that does not support me in being on time or a woman of my word. This belief, or conversation, may be different from person to person and it is up to me to figure out what it is for me. It could be, "I am not that important," "They can start without me" or "I can't be on time." It could be anything that would have "lateness" show up in your space.

The ultimate goal in having what we want and living from our vision is to have our *word* and our *conversations* be aligned with that vision—to have our beliefs generate the actions we desire and have our actions produce the beliefs necessary to sustain those actions. As a result, what you say, do, and promise will then be fully aligned with the beliefs you have about it. This is why Integrity is the first principle of Source Movement. Looking at where you are out of integrity can be used as a tool to uncover what your underlying, limiting conversations are. Furthermore, the practice of being in integrity will begin to shift those same conversations. For instance, if I have a conversation that supports me in being my word, I would be my word. If I have trouble keeping my word, and I make it a point to be a maniac about keeping my promises, it will support me in shifting the conversations about myself that would have me break my word and instead begin to align my stories with someone who is worthy of keeping her word. Practicing being your word is the most powerful tool to alter your stories and beliefs about yourself. Being our word is the highest spiritual practice we can have.

you are ALWAYS in integrity

We are always *in integrity* with something. That is true at all levels of Integrity, and we can use that concept to look at the conversations that have us create the results in our life. In the previous chapter, I told you about a story I used to have about myself: "I never finish anything I start. I will always be just mediocre, never the best or excellent at anything." This story that was not producing the results I wanted was all I was capable of at the time, given my awareness. So all my past results that I was ashamed of or wish never happened were actually completely in integrity with who I "said" I was. It was all in integrity with the conversation that I was. My verbal promise to my ex-wife that I will love her forever was not matching the belief or conversation I had about myself in relationships. By not loving her forever, I was breaking my promise and being out of integrity on one level. At the same time, my results of not loving her forever were in perfect integrity with my conversation about relationships and myself. On an unconscious level, I was saying, "I don't complete anything." Therefore, that is how I was showing up in the relationship. It was more important to me on some level to be "right" about that conversation than to break through and surrender to the commitment I made. I was not aware enough at the time to see the gap between what I said I wanted and what I actually *believed* about it.

This is the key. When we are *out of integrity* with something, we are simultaneously in integrity with something else. The universe is always *in integrity*. So when we agree, for instance, to be somewhere on time and then break our word and show up late, we are *out of integrity* based on the promise we made. At the same time, if we look at what was more important than being on time, we may discover the conversations we were in integrity with to have us not *be our word*. What could those conversations be? It could be as simple as "I can never make it on time" or maybe a deeper conversation such as "I don't matter." Finding the places in your life where you break your word is a powerful way to uncover what your unaligned conversations may be, the ones that don't produce what you say you want. When you break your word, rather than beating yourself up about it, use it as an opportunity to awaken. It is an opportunity to notice where you have unaligned conversations. From that space of awareness, you can then recommit to a future action or possibility that will be aligned with your vision.

Imagine the space that would be opened up if we could align our conversations and stories with our actions that would produce the results we desire. I may have had a vision to create a healthy, joyous marriage that lasted forever, but I was not aware enough to shift the conversations about myself, about her and about marriage that would be in alignment with that vision. Therefore, powerful as I am, I created a result that was in alignment with the story I had. I created a dramatic breakup involving lies and deceit. If I look back at the previous relationships I had, the story pretty much played out the same way. Once I was aware of this and began to look at what possible stories I had about myself, others and about relationships, I started seeing a pattern. I was now able to make some real choices about what was important to me and begin to shift the conversations that were not working. This is where our real power comes in. Our power to create something new! We are creators, after all. We are Source.

Let's explore this more. My friend, Jennifer, was working on renovating her new house. One day she came to the house and noticed that someone broke into her house and stole the copper pipes she just installed. She was devastated. How can we apply this new notion of conversations and Integrity to this event? Let's dissect it and see if we can come up with a formula to empower ourselves rather than falling victim to the events that occur in our lives.

Let's say Jennifer feels deflated and is really bummed someone would do this to her. How could someone be so *out of integrity* that he breaks the law and steals from other people? She had been working so hard to get this new house and put in so much money. Now she has to install new plumbing again and spend more money. Jennifer feels she really does not deserve this, and if she had a chance to catch this thief, she would want to kick his stealing butt. Jennifer spends days talking to her friends about being a victim of a crime and how the world is falling apart. She is now even more concerned about the safety of the neighbor-hood than when she bought the house. She is even talking about selling it and moving somewhere else. She's stressed out because she has spent so much time and money investing in this house.

In this scenario, Jennifer has taken the role of a victim. Most people in the world today would agree with her. I would say, let's not! Let's apply what we just learned about integrity, conversa-tions, and results. So the result is: Jennifer's copper pipes were taken. If we apply the notion that we create all our results out of a conversation or belief we already are, then what could the conversation that Jennifer had about herself and the world be prior to the break-in such that she was a space for it to occur? She brought the event into existence to be right about that story. I know Jennifer, and I know that she has been worried about that neighborhood for a while, and she is always stressed and talks about how the world is taking a turn for the worst. I know people in the same neighborhood who do not have that conver-sation, and they have never had things taken from them. So Jen-nifer's story, her conversation about life, her neighborhood and her stresses, created yet another event that supported her story. Jennifer gets to be right.

If it is so important for us to be right, why don't we start being right about the stuff we really want? What if Jennifer could be aware of her conversations and start shifting them and then take a stand to be right about something that will create what she really wants? What could be possible then?

So how does Integrity fit in with the story about Jennifer? There are several ways we can look at it:

- *The burglar was out of integrity.*

- *The burglar was in integrity.*
- *Jennifer was out of integrity.*
- *Jennifer was in integrity.*

The way our society holds Integrity, we would most likely say that the person who took the pipes was out of integrity. Let's test it against the quote "Source is ALWAYS in integrity, and so am I." This means that both the burglar and Jennifer were in integrity. The question is: in integrity with what? *With the conversations that they are!* The burglar could have a conversation or belief that entitles him or her to take from other people. Jennifer could have a conversation or a belief that has people take from her. Bingo! A match made in heaven! Energetically, they were drawn into each other's experiences because their stories matched like pieces in a puzzle. Wouldn't you love to be at a dinner party with their parrots and listen to them being right?

We have collected all these stories from the past and from our upbringing and environment, and none of them are True with a capital "T." They are just thoughts we have chosen to believe and make true for us. So how do we start changing our stories? That is a great question. Like I mentioned before, we have to become aware of them first. Then we need to look at how we are telling the story. After that, we can begin to generate a different story.

the because—and tool

One thing we often do is collapse the stories with the facts. For instance, in the example about Jennifer, she believed that because her pipes were taken, her neighborhood was bad and the world was coming to an end. She was making the fact and her story about it dependent on each other. One was a result of the other. When we do this, we actually take away our own power to create a different story. This is a very important notion because when we make the fact the cause of our story, the only way to let go of the story is to negate the fact. This does not work. A fact is a fact. The story and the fact need to be separate. So in Jennifer's case, if she were to separate the fact (her pipes were taken) from her story (the neighborhood is bad and the world is coming to an end), she would be free to begin to shift that story without negating the fact that her pipes were stolen. It would sound like this: my pipes were taken and my neighborhood is bad and the world is coming to an end.

I want to dig a lot deeper here and bring this notion into a scenario that may be uncomfortable for you. I am doing this because it is important that we begin to look at some of the bigger events in our lives that we may still have big stories about—stories that could be holding us back. So here it is, you may say, "BECAUSE I was raped, I am not worthy." This statement directly relates your worthiness to the rape. If we break it down, the fact is: You were raped. You are the one directly relating your worthiness to it. That is the story you have about it. Many of us go through our whole life having a story like that from an event in our past where we just simply made up that because something occurred, something else is true. This brings us to a very powerful tool you can use to begin to change your stories. We will call this the "BECAUSE-AND" tool.

Let's use the BECAUSE-AND tool on the example about being raped. First, start by replacing the word BECAUSE with

AND. So instead of saying "BECAUSE I was raped, I am not worthy," we would say, "I was raped, AND I am not worthy." Now you suddenly have a choice, as the event (the fact) and the story are no longer dependent on each other. On one hand, you were raped, AND at the same time, you have a story that says, "I'm not worthy." Now once they are separate, you can change that story. Now you can ask yourself if it is actually true that you are not worthy. You can challenge the story part of the sentence. The second step then would be to change that part to something more empowering: "I was raped, AND I am worthy." There is tremendous power in looking at where you collapse facts with stories by using the word BECAUSE and then changing it to AND, thereby releasing the story from the actual event. Once we do that, we have more freedom to alter the conversations we may have about things.

uncollapsing your stories

Let's dig deeper into the notion of using AND instead of BECAUSE. As we have seen already it is a great tool to use to distinguish the story from the fact, and it takes you one step closer to the awareness that you actually have a story that may not serve you. Sometimes we even use our stories to blame our out of integrity on others. Let's look at the following statements:

- *BECAUSE my husband cheated on me, I am going to keep the children away from their father.*
- *I am not turning my assignment in on time BECAUSE my teacher yelled at me.*
- *I spend most of my time at work doing personal stuff*

BECAUSE my boss is a jerk.
* *I was late BECAUSE of traffic.*

How many times do we blame other people or situations to justify our own lack of integrity? Do we not realize that giving up our own integrity causes us to experience lack of self-worth? It's amazing when we look at how many people don't value their word. They may not see how critical it is to be our word and to follow though on our committed actions. This is what will bring freedom, joy, and self-worth into our lives.

In the previous sentences, looking at the word *because*, we justify being out of integrity by making up "stories" that make it OK for us to break our word. Take for instance, "I was late because of traffic," a very common excuse for being out of integrity. We have now become a victim of traffic. Let's first separate the fact from the circumstance by replacing the word *because* with *and*. "I was late, *and* there was traffic." Now that they are distinct from each other, we can look at each of the statements separately. "I was late"—a fact. "There was traffic"—another fact and also a circumstance. If we are willing to look at what may have been more important than being on time, we may uncover some conversations we have about being on time, about traffic, about ourselves that may not serve us. These could include "I am always late," or if you are on your way to a job interview, "I don't deserve this job."

It can be anything; we all have different stories we tell. How many times do we get in a car knowing that there will be traffic, and we still don't account for the extra time? What if it was possible to alter a conversation you have about it so the relationship you have with the circumstance called "traffic" no longer stops you from being your word? Where do you use other circumstances to blame for the results you have? I know people who are never late, and they drive on the same freeways we do. They have altered their relationship they have between being their word and the circumstances and stories that would have them not be on time. A responsible conversation from our example about traffic could be, "I did not value my word and take the necessary actions to be on time."

Once we get to the place of responsibility and drop the "stories," we can look at WHY we would not value our word and HOW we could be in the future about being our word. We can recommit. I am clear that for me, my word is directly related to my self-worth and in some cases directly related to how I value others' self-worth. Therefore, I value my WORD as my LIFE. It is that important for me. My invitation is: Honor your agreements like your life depends on it—because it does.

When we collapse stories to justify our behaviors, such as "I am not turning in my assignment on time BECAUSE my teacher yelled at me," when one has nothing to do with the other, not only are we compromising our own self-worth and blaming someone else for us being out of Integrity, we could also be validating the other person's lack of self-worth. Imagine the teacher, in this case, has a belief that he is not good enough and directly relates students not turning in assignments on time to his worth as a teacher. Not only do we sell out our own Integrity, but we also get to play a part in validating our teacher's insecurities about not being worthy. Pretty powerful! If you can relate to this, ask yourself, "Is that who I want to be in this world?" Now apply the

Because-And tool, and change the sentence to "I am not turning in my assignment on time AND my teacher yelled at me." This immediately shifts the responsibility from your teacher to you. Now you can own your actions and stories, commit to being in Integrity and stop being a victim.

Because many of our limiting conversations are unconscious, we don't even realize they affect our results. As mentioned before, when we break our word, we have an amazing opportunity to look at where the gap is between being our word and the conversation that would have us break our word. It's an opportunity to really look to see what was more important. I am not talking about the "reasons" you broke your word; I am talking about the conversation you have about yourself that would have you break your word. We are incredible powerful beings. Just by having a conversation of "not good enough," we can create a traffic jam so that we are late, so that we can be right about that we are not worthy of being on time. As Source, we generate all the results, not just the ones we like. Remember the HumanX game and the penny next to a candy wrapper from Chapter 2? We put them both there.

Integrity from a place of "I am always in Integrity with the conversation that I am" can support you in drastically changing the results in your life. You just need to start looking. Once you get this concept, you can use it to become aware of the unconscious beliefs you have so you can shift them if they do not generate what you want. This book is written to have you become aware—to be able to identify these beliefs and make them conscious.

The question now is: Are you willing to not be a victim and

look? Look at the worthiness conversation; look at the deeper stories you made up sometime in your life, the ones that you now spend endless hours, days and years being right about? Are you willing to examine your breakdowns so that you can discover more about yourself and be more aware? Are you ready to begin the exiting journey of creating, of generating, your life, to fully be Source for success in your life and in the world?

There are many ways to have our unconscious beliefs become conscious. Books, exercises, trainings, seminars, and coaching are just a few. Mine were illuminated in the transformational trainings I attended in 2007, and as a result, I practice being my word in all areas of my life. When we begin to complete on our promises and commitments, we honor our word as ourselves and begin to tell a new story: "I am worthy of keeping my commitments." My invitation is to take yourself on! When you are late, LOOK AT WHAT CONTROLS YOU, not from good or bad, but from a neutral place. Your results will tell you what you are in integrity with! At the end of the day, ALL you have is your word; ALL you are is your word. And if your word is WORTH-LESS, then what is YOUR WORTH?

questions for
reflection

1) Do I see myself as a man/woman of my word?

   _____
   _____
   _____

2) Am I attached to my results?

   _____
   _____
   _____

3) Do I refrain from making commitments because of fear I will fail or not measure up?

   _____
   _____
   _____

4) Am I usually on time? If you answered yes to question 1 and no to this question, go back and answer 1 again. It is usually hard to admit that we are not always our word.

   _____
   _____
   _____

call for
action

➲ Commit to being on time for a whole week. Each time you are not
on time, stop for a moment, and look at what other commitments
or conversations were more important. Make a conscious effort not
to be a victim. Honor your results as neutral so you can really look.

➲ Erase the word BECAUSE from your vocabulary for one whole
day. Take some of the stories you have that use BECAUSE, and
replace them with AND. For instance: Because I was fired, I am a
bad employee. Change it to: I was fired, and I am a bad employee.
This is the first step toward uncollapsing a story and taking
responsibility. Now that they are separate, replace the story
("I am a bad employee") with something more empowering.
For example: I was fired, and I can easily get another job.

chapter seven

second principle: responsibility

I create my reality.
This makes me 100 percent responsible
for everything.

his chapter will bring us back to Source. We will explore the principle Responsibility from a stand that we are responsible for everything in our experience, everything in our reality, our game, our movie, everything from our past, present, and future. We are the director, the producer, and the actor. We are not talking about responsibility defined as an obligation, duty or burden as in "my fault" or "I am to blame." We are inviting you to look at and use the distinction of responsibility we present here as a way to *generate* your experience and your future.

Unfortunately, most of us have it ingrained that if we are

responsible, it is a bad thing, like we did something wrong. Imagine all the times growing up when someone would say, "Who is responsible for this?" usually referring to something "bad" that happened. Let go of that way of looking at responsibility. We want to look at Responsibility as a tool, a way to move us toward freedom and power. What could be more powerful then "I am creating everything"? This puts us in a place of creation rather than circumstance, a place of Source rather than victim. Is it true that we create everything? Who knows? Like I explained earlier, it's not necessarily about what is true; it is about what works! Taking responsibility for your life works; it gives you the power to make different choices.

There are different levels of embracing this concept depending on how far you want to take it. Personally, I believe I am the only one out there; I am part of the all; I am the author; I generate it all. Starting out this way may be a foreign concept, so let's see if we can look at it in a different way and still have it be profoundly powerful in your life.

Let's start by saying that you are the creator of your own *internal* experience. You are in charge of your feelings and your emotions. I'm sure you can accept that notion. Think about it; you are always the one there when you are having these experiences. Who is always there when you are anxious, angry or annoyed? YOU! So if you can accept that you are the one in charge of your emotions, feelings and reactions, you certainly could be in charge of shifting them to something more effective, something that would give you joy and peace rather than anxiety and despair.

Imagine you are in the midst of an emotional, messy situation that is taking up all your energy and time and is making you depressed and angry. You may ask, "How can I feel joy and peace in the midst of this? Who am I to laugh when my world is falling apart?" I firmly believe that it is more than possible to walk through something like this in a state of joy. All our feelings and emotions are generated from our thoughts about the events, not necessarily the events themselves. For instance, my friend's mother died from a disease when my friend was 6 years old, and as a result, her life was "ruined." She would always bring up her sadness and how unfair it was and how her life would have been so much better if her mom was still alive. Who is responsible for my friend's life being absolute crap because her mom died? She is! Not the event, nor God, nor anyone else. Could she take responsibility for the stories she made up? Could she let them go and make up stories that would have brought her joy and power despite her mother's death?

are you "in it" or "of it"?

You may wonder if it is bad to have an experience of anxiety, sadness or anger. Absolutely not! We are human beings, and we are feeling machines! Taking responsibility causes you to move from being a victim to a place of choice and power. May you still choose to stay angry and sad? You may! We are not suggesting you should not experience your experience; we want to give you power to move toward *having an experience* rather than the *experience having you.*

Is it possible to have an experience of fear and not be fear? When you are in a sticky situation and you feel out of control or feel like a victim to what is happening, ask yourself, "Is it possible for me to be 'in' it rather than be 'of' it?" By simply asking yourself that question, you have established that there is a distinction between the two and that you have a choice. Can I be *in* a divorce and not *become* the divorce?

I am sure you have had an experience when a situation consumes you. For instance, you become the breakup, the rape, or the accident, and you begin to identify with it. Most of the time, we do this to get the juicy payoffs of being a victim. This usually happens on an unconscious level. Our society is very talented at feeling sorry for one another and giving all kinds of attention to people in despair. Unfortunately, as you may have experienced, the good feeling of "pity" does not last too long. In fact, it isn't real and authentic anyway, and on some level, you know that. So again, the question is: Can you walk through the valley of the shadow of death and not *BE* the valley of the shadow of death? Can you experience joy and peace in the midst of a rough spot?

If you think about it, most of the time, the event is just that: an event. It is neutral. For instance, there are tribes in this world that completely embrace and celebrate the death of a member of their family. They actually experience joy when a person dies. In most western countries, many people see death as something awful and sad. Most of us grieve for weeks, months, and sometimes years. So what is it? Is death a bad thing or a good thing? It is neutral. Neither of the worldviews on death is right or wrong. And you don't necessarily have to change your worldview. What I am saying, however, is that you are the one choosing your feelings and beliefs, and if you are choosing them, why not choose what will bring you inner peace and joy?

The first step to be able to choose joy and peace in any

situation is to take ownership of how you view the situation. Own everything you are feeling, thinking, expressing, saying and doing. This will have you separate yourself from the actual event or situation, and it generates a space for you to make some important choices. If you are on automatic and reacting to the event, you have no power. The event has your power. Once you are clear and in charge of your thoughts, feelings and emotions, you can begin to shift them. The second step toward peace and joy is—if you are willing to go this far—to take full responsibility for everything that is occurring and be willing to own that you have set up the whole situation for one reason only: to awaken.

Remember the HumanX game we talked about in the beginning of the book? Let's play a little with that notion. The events in your past are simply an obstacle course created for you to move though in order to fully play the game—to be able to experience all the ups and downs of humanity. Let's imagine each event is part of the contract card drawn from the game board. The events on the cards are drawn and assigned to each human as part of the game to have us doubt ourselves as the creator, as Source. The game would be no fun if you knew immediately that you were the creator, if you figured it out right away (although some of us actually do know this from birth). Since the humans in the HumanX game have free will and an ego, there is no way for the *being* playing the game, your higher self, to know which event or at what time you will have a moment of awakening, a moment of getting who you really are. This is why it is so much fun to play the game in the first place. As each human begins to be aware and awaken, he or she will have more fun within the game, find peace and joy, and begin to deliberately create his or her future.

As awakening occurs, there is an opening created where our higher selves, who are playing the game, can begin to communicate with their humans and thereby assisting them in the process of awakening. This communication can take different forms and is not guaranteed. Some of us may hear a voice guiding us, or in other cases, it may show up as signs that we begin to notice or ask for. For others, it is more of a *knowing,* a sense of connectedness to something beyond ourselves. It does not matter what it looks like as it usually produces the same result: a sense of oneness and inner peace—a feeling that all is well and you experience gratitude for everything. Responsibility on this level is an *ability to respond* to this oneness and realize that within it, you have the power to create.

You may now wonder how it is that we just claimed that you create EVERYTHING when in the scenario from the HumanX game a card drawn randomly from a game board determines the events. How can we claim that you created those events? Well, here is where our brilliance as creators comes in: we also created the card that was drawn! It's pretty simple; we design the cards, sit down and play the game, draw the cards randomly so we won't know what card we will draw, and then play using that card as if the events generated are real. On some level, we forget that we created it in the first place, so we think all these events are happening to us, rather than for and by us. Charles Darrow, who created Monopoly, did just that. He designed a game that he could also sit down and play without knowing the outcome. He would not know when he would draw a "Go to Jail" card. He may even get upset if he does, even though he designed that specific card and the results generated from drawing the card.

I had a dream once where I was standing in line at a coffee shop. Suddenly, this man came up behind me, and because I didn't see him, I was startled. In my dream I had all the physical reactions of being startled. My heart skipped a beat, my body jumped, and I was short of breath. I woke up, and my body was still startled. Who was the one dreaming this dream? I was! Who was the one being startled? I was! How can I startle *myself*? Who is the *I*? Who is the *myself*? I then realized that if I can create a dream that has me startled as if I didn't know what was happening, then would it not be possible for that same *I* to create a game that the *myself* is playing with all the surprises and events occurring without knowing it is not real and it is just a game? Isn't it then also possible that you can *create* a traffic jam, make yourself *forget* you created it, drive into it, and then get furious and flip the bird at the other drivers as if it is real and happening to you? Think about that for a moment. . . .

Stand if you get it. I mean it—stand up for a second if you get it. Physically changing your body when you grasp or learn something can give you an anchor to remember what you learned. You can sit down now.

My invitation is this: However you get there, get to a place where you can be authentically responsible for how you act, feel, think and create in all situations. If it is difficult for you to say that you are the one who created the rape happening or your mother dying, you don't need to. However, do take responsibility for all the stories you have made up about it, and be open to the notion that those stories could have you be the space for other similar events happening. Own those stories, and change them if they don't bring you joy and peace. Responsibility holds power and freedom. If that is what you want, be willing to be 100 percent responsible 100 percent of the time.

questions for
reflection

1) How have I played a victim in my life?

_____

_____

2) Have you had dreams that startled you?

_____

_____

3) What are the events that have been on your Human
   X contract card so far?

_____

_____

_____

4) How are you speaking about those events?

_____

_____

_____

5) Can you think of a situation when you were able
   to be "in" it and not "of" it?

_____

_____

_____

call for
action

⊃ Take a situation where you believe you are or were a victim, and tell the story from a completely responsible view. Don't sell out on yourself. There is always a responsible version to all our stories. If it feels inauthentic, do it anyway. Have some fun with it. If you need coaching, get it.

⊃ Ask three close friends or people you trust if they see you as responsible or a victim. Ask people who will be honest with you. Ask for examples to back up their assessment. Be open. This could be the first step in uncovering an unconscious belief. You could have a blind spot here that does not serve you. Remember that it is not BAD if they see you as a victim. It is just how you have been showing up. If it serves you, keep it. If you see that it may not, begin to shift your story about it. Begin to take actions and have conversations that support you in being responsible.

third principle: gratitude

*I am grateful for EVERYTHING.
I celebrate ALL my results equally with
gratitude and awe.*

g ratitude is the principle I hold nearest to my heart. When we stand in a place of gratitude, our lives are richer. Gratitude is the highest state of consciousness. Gratitude brings us to the present moment, and it creates an egoless space. It is the foundation of all abundance.

I look at Gratitude as a state of being and a state of mind. It is a state, similar to joy, in which we have an understanding (or a deep connection) that everything is as it should be, and we are grateful that it is. Gratitude is the highest level of consciousness in taking full responsibility as Source. When we can accept everything as being exactly as it should be and at the same time stand in gratitude for it, we begin to manifest peace and love.

I want to make a distinction here between thankfulness and Gratitude. Being thankful is usually generated and expressed from a situation, circumstance or condition; whereas, Gratitude is simply a state of being, regardless of those things. Thankfulness is more like "doing gratitude" rather than "being gratitude." For instance, I may be thankful that I did not run out of gas on my way home from work and grateful there is even something called gas that can make my car move. Being grateful is when you look at the whole rather than the specific situation. Many times, thankfulness and gratitude are used synonymously, and I don't see a reason to go too deep here about the difference. I think the best description of Gratitude is what we said in the beginning of this paragraph worth reiterating: Gratitude is a state of consciousness in which we have an understanding (or a deep connection) that everything is as it should be, and we are grateful that it is.

So how do we be Gratitude no matter what? How do we become grateful for EVERYTHING? Gratitude consciousness does not necessarily just appear; although, it can. For some, it is a state toward which to work. I believe that "doing gratitude" and being thankful for the people and things around us will put us on the right path toward a state of gratitude. Moreover, becoming aware of our unaligned conversations and limiting beliefs will certainly support us in the process. We have given you some tools and concepts so far in this book that can support you in becoming aware and begin to live a life in integrity, from a responsible point of view and as Source. This chapter and our next two chapters about service and community will provide more grounds toward living a life in gratitude.

my path to gratitude

I want to share my personal journey of gratitude and how it became a way of life for me. Your path toward gratitude may look completely different, so I invite you to look for the nuggets that may support you in your personal quest for gratitude and peace.

I was born and raised in Sweden. Although gratitude as a concept or as a word was not discussed much in my family, there was always a sense of thanksgiving for the things we had. Somewhere inside I knew I was fortunate. The sense of gratitude was handed to me from my family, and even though it was more on a conditional level—"I am grateful because I have something"—I was able to get a sense of deeper gratitude. I understood that not only was I fortunate, we ALL were, no matter what. Because of this, I was mostly a happy kid and a pretty joyous teenager. Of course I had trials and tribulations of any teenager growing up in an upper-class community outside Stockholm. The alcohol was abundant both for the adults and the teenagers, and I had a tremendous amount of freedom that I gladly took advantage of, which led me to many hard lessons learned. Note to self: Don't drive a moped without a headlight in the middle of the night while intoxicated, and don't schedule a tennis date with mom at 8 a.m. after a party where you fell and broke your wrist (although, I must say, I almost got away with it playing with my left hand).

When I turned 20, I decided I wanted to go to college in America. I ended up in Virginia at Randolph-Macon Woman's College, and a year later, I moved to Los Angeles to attend Loyola Marymount University. The next 15 years I spent chasing the

American Dream while jumping from relationship to relationship and enjoying one too many drinks on the weekends. From
the outside, I was successful and happy, and people wanted to
be around me. On the inside, I was slowly dying. Was this it?
What am I missing here? I felt as if I was constantly running, as
if where I was just was not good enough. I was haunted by my
upbringing of always having to be the best, and yet, even then,
I never felt good enough. Life was mediocre. I was mediocre. At
least that's how I saw it then. My belief system was set in stone.

At 36, I moved to Florida, attended a transformational workshop and had a life-changing moment of gratitude at an airport
with Don Warms (see Chapter 3 for the full story). When I committed to giving out a Token of Appreciation every day to someone I was grateful for, in what I called the Giving Year, I had no
idea I was on my journey toward a purpose-filled life in joy and
gratitude.

It was during the Giving Year, and especially toward the
end of it, that I realized everything I had been asking for and
declared was manifesting right in front of my eyes. I was creating
the relationships I wanted, my career was taking off, and joy was
becoming a natural state of being. This is when I really "got"
the importance of giving and receiving and the importance of
gratitude.

I wanted to share this personal discovery with the world. I
realized there was actually a recipe for living in joy, and the base
ingredient was gratitude! Sounds pretty simple, no? Well, it is—if
you are a clear space and an opening to be gratitude.

Let me explain. Gratitude is ultimately a state of being. In a
state of gratitude, one is completely present to the now. When we

choose to be grateful, fear, judgment, and scarcity move out of our consciousness. This is the part that can be tough for some of us; it was for me—at least before I had done some serious self-reflecting by attending personal development and transformational trainings. Think about it, I had 36 years of belief systems and conversations that had me spinning my wheels and re-creating the same experiences over and over. I was getting nowhere. And if you had told me back then to be grateful for it all, I would have knocked you over the head with a frying pan!

the three steps

Let's explore three steps that will move you into a state of gratitude and support you to authentically be grateful for EVERYTHING.

Step 1: Awareness

In order to have a chance at a life in gratitude, we need to become aware of our unconscious beliefs. Sounds like a catch-22, I know! How do I become aware of something unconscious? Well, there are many ways. This book is one of them. Other ways include workshops, therapy, reading books, life coaching etc. The most powerful way I have seen to date is the Gratitude Training. Part 1 of this training is designed to have you see "how you do you." Through a myriad of exercises, games, group work and lectures, the training illuminates your blind spots, and you get a clear idea of what beliefs work for you and the ones that don't. Most of us don't even realize that there are millions of things we don't even know about ourselves or what we are capable of.

This limitation has us operate from the same "box" and create the same results in our life. Awareness that there is another possibility and that we have endless choices in our life is the first step toward a life in gratitude.

Step 2: Clear out the junk

The second step is the most powerful step and the step most of us resist to face. It is about being willing to own our ugly side, or what some authors now call, our shadow side. If you think you don't have one, you are lying to yourself. Jump back to Step 1 and do some more awareness work! We all have it: wrong-minded thinking, a shadow side, things we are not proud of, beliefs that have us act like we are completely mad. I call it junk. It is important to realize that having junk is not bad; it is merely your conversations that don't serve you. We already talked about this in Chapter 5. After becoming aware of all these conversations and beliefs, we have an opportunity to break through and clear out what is not serving us in our life anymore. When I say "clear out the junk," I am referring to accepting the junk and not having it run us anymore, rather than forgetting or getting rid of it. Part 2 of the Gratitude Training is designed to do just that. It creates a safe environment for you to break though anything that has stopped you in your life, all in a five-day training. If you are now thinking that I am "selling" you the Gratitude Training, you are right! I am! I promise you it is the most powerful self-actualization work you will find. I am so confident about it that I give you all your money back after Part 2 if this is not true for you. Regardless of how you decide to clear out the junk, do it! I am on your team.

Step 3: Be the change you want to see

This step, the final one, is about living a life in integrity with your principles, your values. It is about being diligent about what you are doing and how you are being. In this step, you take the awareness from step 1 and the acceptance from step 2 and begin to apply it in your life. Think about it. How are you "showing up" in your life? What do people say about you? What is the spirit in your family? Are you keeping your word? The third step is mainly about two fundamental distinctions: commitment and forgiveness. As I am sure you agree, we could probably write several books about mastering these two distinctions. We will keep it simple without compromising the essence and importance. We will look at commitment as the fuel for our vision and our goals. When we commit to our word, our principles and our self, we begin to move toward manifesting what we say we want, our vision. Sound easy enough? Well, unfortunately, what has us break our commitment most of the time are those unaligned conversations and limiting beliefs we spoke about earlier. Many people don't even like to commit to anything at all because the fear of failure (or success) is so prevalent. Yet, when we consistently take committed action, are willing to fail and recommit, and are ready to accept success, we begin to live a life of value—to others, the world and ourselves. Forgiveness is closely related to gratitude because it is about fully accepting what is, what has been and what may happen. Forgiveness is not about acknowledging that someone did something to you that you forgive him or her for; it is about acknowledging that there is nothing and no one to be forgiven . . . ever. Forgiveness is giving of yourself fully, allowing the essence of you emerge and be shared. When we hold grudges or experience guilt, we block this love from being brought forth. So rather than focusing on what we may want to forgive someone for, we can instead give forth our love and authenticity, with a knowingness that there is nothing that needs to be "set straight," "rectified" or "forgiven."

We tend to waste so much energy when we spend time "hanging out" in guilt or intolerance. We waste so much energy that we can't even imagine having time to set goals and committing to them. This is why being the change requires you to master the distinctions of commitment and forgiveness; so that you can free up space to declare, commit and manifest a big vision and at the same time feel complete peace when you have setbacks and disappointments.

The third and final part of Gratitude Training is called Masterful Living. It is a three-month leadership program designed to have you master your life and become a leader in your family, community and the world. It is all about being the change you want to see and about being a contribution. We don't always realize it, but many of us have lived as leeches our whole life, trying to get something from life, rather than to give and contribute to it. When we can make giving a habit, we begin to have all that we ever wanted.

Let's reiterate the three steps that will support you to be a clear space to authentically move gratitude through you in the present moment and fully experience joy. First, figure out a way to become aware of your unconscious beliefs. Be willing to uncover the ones that are limiting and stop you from your heartfelt desires and goals. Second, clear out the junk! Once you are aware of what is not working for you, break through these limiting beliefs, and begin to experience freedom and power. Third, put it into practice. The only way to reform habits is by continuously doing it for more than two months (according to a study by Phillippa Lally at University College London). By instilling commitment and forgiveness into our practices, we bring value to life, and in turn, we become the change we want to see in the world.

These three steps will bring you to a complete new level of consciousness. You become a new environment, or context, for new results to flourish. I call this The Gratitude Context. None of these steps will inherently make you "happy." What will create a sense of joy inside your being is when you naturally move into a state of gratitude, which is also a state of NOW, being fully present. This is where the good stuff begins. This is where it gets fun! Life explodes right in front of your eyes. Your whole environment shifts into a state of abundance. Abundance of love, peace, relationships, finances—whatever it is you want! For me personally, my vision is to create gratitude and joy wherever I go. If I find that I am not, I use the three steps to see what I can shift to get back to my vision. I simply ask myself, "Who do I want to be?"

The ancient Roman statesman and philosopher Cicero once said, "Gratitude is not only the greatest of virtues, but a parent of all the others." Eckhart Tolle is one of many who claim that gratitude is the Source of all abundance. When we are truly grateful, our vibration heightens, and we start attracting other grateful people, experiences, and things. Furthermore, when we move into a state of gratitude, we tend to hold other people high, bringing forth and drawing out the greatness and beauty in them. We are now being a context (an environment) for others and ourselves living from a space of love, peace, and abundance. As a result, simply by being grateful, we can transform the world. Next time you catch yourself in fear or judgment, remind yourself that your state of being creates the world around you. Do you want to create war, fighting, and scarcity, or do you want to be the Source for love, peace, and gratitude? The moment you authentically shift from fear to love, you will notice how all the things that upset you disappear (and in some cases become humorous!). Use gratitude to make this shift.

One of the Call for Action items at the end of this chapter is to not complain for one full day. The invitation is to choose gratitude for one whole day and watch as the world around you transforms. A friend asked me once, "Being that you now are in a state of gratitude, do you still get mad and want to yell at bad drivers like you used to?" It suddenly dawned on me... There are no bad drivers anymore! They have vibrated out of my consciousness. Where gratitude resides, anger, judgment, and fear cannot. I have actually changed the world around me by living in gratitude and by changing my thoughts!

There are many ways to move toward a state of gratitude. For some of us, it is simply a choice that is made in every present moment, or it can be something we work toward in our personal development and as we try to identify and create our purpose in life. I believe it is related to self-worth and understanding that we are whole, perfect, and complete, and that each situation is occurring exactly as it is supposed to. If we are "in" a situation and detach from the circumstance of it (not be "of" it), we can then view it as an opportunity to see and learn something about ourselves as we move through it with gratitude and a joy-filled heart.

questions for
reflection

1) Where in my life do I choose fear, judgment and scarcity over love, acceptance and abundance?

_____

_____

_____

2) Do I tend to hold resentment and grudges?

_____

_____

_____

3) What am I thankful for?

_____

_____

_____

4) What am I grateful for?

_____

_____

_____

5) Am I willing to be grateful for EVERYTHING?

_____

_____

_____

6) How does gratitude show up in my life? Is it present, absent, sporadic?

_____

_____

_____

call for
action

- ➲ No complaining for one full day. This is a fun challenge! For one full day, choose to not complain about anything. Be rigorous. Do not think, speak or act out your complaints; simply drop them all together. If you catch yourself complaining, add another day to your challenge! If you can authentically be in gratitude for one full day, you will have an experience of peace.

- ➲ Forgive or give forth. Write down a list of everyone and anything you have resentment toward or any grudges you have. Be willing to see your part in any situation. Remember coming from Source: I author everything. When you are complete, read it again, and be willing to give forth love to all of it, realizing that it is a reflection of your current consciousness at the time, and be grateful that in this moment you can shift it. When we hold on to old incidents, we are holding on to that old level of consciousness. Let it go. When you feel complete and clear of judgment, fear and resentment, dispose of the list however you feel would serve you best. Make a commitment to extend love to everyone and everything on your list.

- ➲ Pick someone in your life for whom you are grateful, and express your gratitude to him or her. Don't say you are completing a challenge or reading a book about gratitude; simply share how you feel. If you want to take this to the next level, find something you are grateful for in the person you are least grateful for, and share it with him or her. This can be the beginning of transforming your relationship with that person—or at least changing the stories you have made up about it. After all, you are a space for them to be this way for a reason!

➲ Sign up for the Gratitude Training. Don't take this lightly. The Gratitude Training is not for the faint of heart. It is a serious commitment to yourself. You will be challenged on many levels and in all areas of your life. You have to be ready. If you are ready, make the commitment, and dive in fully. The life possible at the end of the program is unimaginable. If Gratitude Training is not in your cards at this time, make a commitment to the three steps to a life of gratitude and joy, and find the means and tools to get there.

chapter nine

fourth principle: service

Through complete surrender,
I am in selfless service to others and the world.

One day, my wife, Arian, was sick and asked me if I could pick up some cranberry juice on my morning walk. When I got to the juice aisle, I noticed there were all kinds of different flavored cranberry juices: cran-apple, cran-pomegranate, cran-raspberry, etc. I thought to myself, "Wow, I bet the cran-pomegranate is delicious." I grabbed it thinking that she would rather have that and she would be happy with my choice. As I was walking to the cash register, it suddenly hit me. She asked for cranberry juice, not a variation of it. I was putting my own spin on it and making up stories to back up what I really wanted. This hit me like a lightning bolt. How often was I doing that? How often was I asked to do or be something and then changed it to what I decided it meant or what I wanted? I suddenly saw so many instances where I controlled the outcome of others' requests and desires. I thought about all my past romantic relationships and was suddenly clear why they did not work. Anyway, I returned the cran-pomegranate and grabbed what she asked for: plain cranberry juice. When I got home and mentioned that I had almost bought the cran-pomegranate, she said, "Oh, I don't like that one at all!"

As I was sitting here writing about her and the juice, she handed me a list of groceries to pick up. Ten minutes later, she asked me to cross out apple juice and add orange juice. I responded, "You can have both; why don't I get both?" I DID IT AGAIN! I wanted to adjust her request! She said very clearly, cross out the apple and add orange. Why would I think she would say that if she wanted both? We could argue that I am trying to be giving and considerate, but if we really look at it, all I am doing is putting my spin on it, and in doing so, I belittle her as if she does not know what she wants. Wow, you can learn a lot from juice!

In earlier chapters, we have talked a lot about our conversations or stories that we have. It is incredibly powerful to become aware of them because most of the time they are making decisions for us. In the previous examples about juice, I became aware of how in my past, I would let my own preferences and beliefs make the decisions, even at the expense of others. We tend to listen through the filters of our beliefs and then make up, or interpret, what is offered or requested so it serves our own agenda. We do this unconsciously. We constantly put our own spin on life. There is no problem putting your own spin on things if you are consciously doing it and it is aligned with your bigger vision.

However, many of us do it without even realizing it. We are acting on autopilot, which strips us of our personal power and ability to create what we want. Once we become aware and are able to catch ourselves when we fall into our *automatic*, we can begin to take actions that will benefit the greater vision, rather then reacting to past events and beliefs. This requires a new level of surrender for many of us. When we become aware and begin to act from a true place of service to the world and our vision, we begin to hear the needs of others and a new willingness to serve is born. We were all born with an innate desire to make a difference in the world through giving and receiving. When we forget this desire and begin to worry about our own personal gain, sometimes at the expense of others, we begin to drain our families, communities and ultimately the world of all the resources that are available for an abundant, peaceful world to exist. When we are in service, we awaken and are the Source of this new possibility of a harmonious, abundant Earth.

Being in service is the ultimate in SURRENDER. The surrender of beliefs we have about control, time, money—all the conversations that fuel us on a daily basis. When you are in service, true selfless service, to another human being or to a community, you open up a space for abundance to flow through you and through the one you're serving. The gratitude generated from you being in service is fuel for gratitude in your life, and gratitude is the foundation of abundance!

I want to share another example from my life. As I am writing this book, every day there is something that occurs that makes me realize how important the distinction of being in service is in our personal and romantic relationships. I had another experience with my wife on a regular Saturday morning. I woke up to her manically cleaning the house. She had been sick for about a week and had hit that point of "I need to clean out the sickness." She was washing blankets, vacuuming and dusting everywhere. My agenda for this Saturday morning was very different than the one she had begun. I decided the night before that I would wake up, have coffee and then write a few more pages of this book. I was lying in bed listening to her banging around and making loud noises. It was as if I could hear her saying the following through every loud noise: "Why isn't Jo helping me? I have been sick, and she is just sleeping."

I was dreading getting up. I was working myself up into a frenzy about how I should just do what I had decided and keep my commitment to myself and that if she wanted to clean now, that was her choice; my schedule was important, too... blah blah blah... Then I stopped for a second. I started thinking about what I had been writing about and about surrender. What was my real commitment here? What was most important to me? I asked myself what it would take from me to surrender completely and go out and be in service to Arian and still have my other commitments happen. In that moment I got it. I got that by surrendering to her, my most important commitment, I opened up a space of love and acceptance that was not possible from the place I was standing prior. I jumped out of bed and embraced Arian in the kitchen as she asked me if I could help. I said I would love to, and we cleaned the house together for an hour and a half while having fun and joking around. I had more time than I could have imagined to still complete on my other commitments, and there was even time to spare! What a lesson!

What would life be like if we completely surrendered to be in service at all times. What if we completely surrendered to what was asked of us without putting our own spin on it or come up with a different solution or way of being in service? What if someone asked you to go to the store and buy ice cream and you simply just said, "Sure, no problem" and left immediately. What would be possible if we just let go and serve?

We are all very sneaky. We know so many different ways of avoiding surrender—avoiding being in service to another human being or to the world. Most of the time, our ego, our stories, and our laziness get in the way. There are many factors that will have us refrain from being in true service. For example: "I am too tired," "I know better how this should be done," "I don't have the time," "They should pay someone to do this," etc. If we really took a look at what was underneath these assessments, we would most likely find the environment or space from which most of us live our lives. It is a context of fear, scarcity, and circumstance. When we are in selfless service, we actually begin to shift those conversations, and instead, gratitude and abundance begin to flow into our consciousness and our lives. If you know you have stories or conversations like the ones just mentioned, find a place to be in service that forces you to let them go. It is when we are in service that we open up a space of gratitude, love, forgiveness, and abundance in our lives and in the world.

Most of the time, our beliefs and conversations have us not be present to listen to what is requested of us. We have already figured out the answer, worked out the solution, or have already made up that we are not good enough to handle the task, and we become an automatic "no." What if we actually execute all requests made of us exactly the way they are made without hearing it through our listening filters without controlling it. What would be possible then? What would we create?

Some of you may wonder at this point, "What about when I need to say no? What about boundaries?" Let's look at that. It is important that we remember that we have all the power. When we talk about surrendering, we are talking about surrendering to our commitments. So if you make a commitment to serve, serve from a place of surrender. If you are committed to love, love from a place of surrender. If you are committed to creating peace, surrender to the journey, and don't try to control the results. When asked to be in service, ask yourself, "Will this serve my vision and align with my principles?" If the answer is yes, consider accepting the request. If the answer is no, you may or may not accept, depending on if you are available.

There is tremendous power in being fully engaged and surrendered once you have committed. Service projects and being in service to another human being is an amazing platform to learn about surrender. If we can learn to surrender to a commitment from a place of peace, we begin to create amazing results. For instance, if you have kids, you know about surrender. If your baby wakes up in the middle of the night with a high fever, it does not matter how tired you are or whatever the circumstances you have, you get up and take care of your baby. You surrender to your commitment of being a parent. We do this all the time in our lives; we have many moments of surrendering to our commitments. What if it was possible to surrender to EVERYTHING we commit to, such as going to the gym, losing weight, getting a new job, making more money? What could we create then? Imagine holding our commitment to going to the gym as important as getting up and caring for our baby.

We constantly hold commitment and being our word at different levels of importance. It is a way for us to "get away with" not keeping our promises and justify it so we won't feel bad about it. This all brings us back to integrity and our stories! Being in service will bring all our conversations to the surface, and it is an opportunity to break through them and find peace. Once we learn how to fully be in service from a place of complete surrender, we will know what love and peace really are. Our own life will begin to thrive, as will the community and people we are serving. Everyone wins.

questions for
reflection

1) Where do I put different importance on my commitments and my word?

_____

_____

_____

2) When I am asked to do something, to be in service, do I do it with joy and peace?

_____

_____

_____

3) Do I put my own spin on everything? Really look here.

_____

_____

_____

4) When was the last time I was in service to a larger community?

_____

_____

_____

5) When was the last time I was in service to my loved ones?

_____

_____

_____

6) Do I ever use my stories about "boundaries" to justify not being in service? We are not talking about the legitimate "no" here.

_____

_____

_____

call for
action

➲ Be in complete service to everyone for one full day. Pick a day when you honor all the requests that are made of you. Do not tell anyone this is what you are doing. Feel free to offer your services, as well.

➲ Find a community service project or a volunteer shift, and donate three hours of your time. Work on not being attached to what the service is. If you find that you are attached to what you may do for the three hours, have someone else pick it for you.

chapter ten

fifth principle: community

*A community is where we express our oneness
and co-create peace, love, and joy.*

So far we have talked about how we create every-thing. This is also true for Community. We create the community or communities we choose to be part of. For the purpose of our discussion, we will describe Community as "a network or group of collaborating people with a common vision." When we find a group of people with a similar vision, we open up a space for our collective consciousness to interact, and we begin to co-create together. This supports us individually and as a whole. On some level, the members of a community together *decide and align* with what is important to that specific community. When individuals align with the vision, language and the practices of a specific group they may choose to join or identify with it. This is how communities are born.

In order to successfully live by the four principles we have explored so far, it is essential that we have an environment that cultivate our growth and our vision. Because the main goal of writing this book is to create world peace in our lifetime by encouraging you to live by the principles of Source Movement, we will specifically refer to communities whose main goal is to make a difference in the world. A thriving community is the perfect space for us to be in service, to experience and give gratitude, to practice being in integrity, and to watch our results as we stand as responsible for everything. Without a community, we stand little chance to live fully expressed and from an authentic place of giving.

A Community is a context—an environment that is created for the purpose of furthering its individuals and the group as a whole toward a vision. It can be as simple as people aligning behind a sports team winning a season or extended like an online social network like Facebook. I have been part of many different communities in my lifetime. Anything from being an avid New York Jets fan to the gay and lesbian communities in the various places I have lived. Whether it was winning a game or advocating gay marriages, I never realized how important it was for me to align with people toward a common goal. This brings me back to going to a Jets game and seeing 30,000 people doing the "wave." Those moments when all of us are aligned to create magic always bring me to tears. It brings a natural high, an experience of pure joy and connection. We all have moments like that; for some they are few and sporadic, and for others they are becoming a way of life. What about for you? What are your moments of pure joy and connection? When we know what they are, we can create more of them.

Unfortunately, over time, our society has become very skeptical to any organization or community that creates these moments of joy on a regular basis. This makes me laugh! Many of us think that "it is too good to be true" or that "joy like that can't happen" and it must be "inauthentic," or "something must be wrong," and we begin attacking and judging it rather than opening up a space of learning.

I want to bring this up because this is another moment where we can retrain our parrot. Sometimes our parrot becomes bitter and skeptical over the years. My invitation here is this: When something seems too good to be true, open up a space to believe it is true, and try it on. If it turns out otherwise, you must have wanted it that way because of some internal conversation you have. Many times, out of fear of bringing our unaligned conversations to light, we'd rather sit back, judge, and attack. When you find yourself attacking or judging, stop for a moment and see if you can figure out what is underneath the judgment or the attack. What are the thoughts and beliefs that would make it safer to choose attack and judgment over acceptance and love? Wherever there is attack, defense, and judgment, there is fear. What are you afraid of?

Let's look at an example. Some of you have heard about CrossFit. It is a strength and conditioning fitness program that's quickly grown in popularity in America. It has created a huge community of likeminded individuals with a common goal: to be fit and healthy. I have never tried it, but it looks like it

works. One day, a new CrossFit gym opened on a road I travel
frequently. I remember driving by it and seeing them all doing
some boot-camp-like exercises, and my parrot immediately said,
"That is just a fad. People don't really work out that way. It does
not work. They should worry more about what they eat...blah
blah blah..."

Now, why would my parrot say that? And more importantly,
why would I choose to believe it? Here is why: I had not worked
out in more than six months (not typical for me) and as a result
gained some weight. I've gone back and forth between different
types of exercise and can't seem to generate consistency. My parrot was taught early on to remind me that no matter what I do,
I'll always have my grandmother's fat thighs. Because of these
internal conversations, it would be too scary to even be open
to the fact that CrossFit will work for me. If I were to accept
that it would, I'd have to really get out of my comfort zone and
take some action. Not only that—what if I held it as true? That
CrossFit will work for me? And then didn't find time to execute
their schedule. I'd fail before even starting! I would also have to
be willing to be wrong about the stories my parrot has been telling me. Wrong about my story about my fat thighs and that they
are, in fact, perfect and can take to exercise as well as any part of
my body. Now that is scary! That means that if I actually have fat
thighs, it's because I am choosing it, not because someone told
me so. Looking at all this, it is actually "safer" and "easier" to
just drive by and judge it—that is why we tend to believe our parrot. However, that will not create what I want in my life. Staying
safe and in fear will not create extraordinary results. What it will
do, however, is have me point fingers at success and happiness

and say, "That is too good to be true." It will have me operate from fear. It will have me be a coward.

So why am I bringing this up in the chapter on Community? It is because a community can be our biggest savior and the biggest threat to our parrot. The CrossFit community was a clear threat to my stories, and my parrot made sure she told me. Once I become aware of these conversations and aware of what my parrot usually will say, I have a choice in how to be and what actions to take. In this case, I was able to hold up on the judgments and instead appreciate and honor the CrossFit community and all the great they do in the world! Does it mean that I have to join their gym right away? No, yes, maybe.... that is not the point. The awareness of my judgment had me look at the conversations I had around my weight and my fitness, and opened up a space to shift those conversations. This is what will ultimately have me shift my weight (with some action, of course). Ultimately, I had CrossFit work for me without even going into the building!

A community that is aligned with what you want will support you in choosing from vision rather than from your stories and your circumstances. Earlier in the chapter, I mentioned that we are specifically referring to communities that are aligned to make a difference in the world. Regardless of the community you choose to associate with, check in with yourself to make sure it will forward you as a leader and contributor. A community is not just there for you to get a sense of belonging (although, most of the time it will); it is there so you can step into your biggest self and be a contribution to others. Since you are the one creating the community, if you find yourself in one that does not enhance your life and the world, you want to shift some of your own beliefs so you have the power to create the community in which you want to co-create.

In the past, I was never a big participant in my community; just belonging to one generated security and a sense of belonging and joy for me. Today this notion has drastically changed for me. I now know that through team and community, we can begin to change the world. It is no longer all about me or about how I can use the community for my personal gain or get happiness from it. It's about how I can serve, how I can be a contribution. The most thriving communities have members who are in service and understand that an aligned vision of the community is the key to abundance for all. I am now awake to what is possible when people come together in integrity, responsibility, gratitude and service to manifest a common vision that is in service to the planet.

So if there are all kinds of communities, how do I pick the one that will forward me to manifest a specific vision? I say, find people who have a similar vision, and surrender to that vision by being willing to let go of your ego and your personal agenda. There is no need to reinvent the wheel; the community you are searching for is right there in front of you. Your stories about communities, service and collaboration will present the community you are ready to join. So if you think you want to find a community that will change the world and you have a conversation and a fear that things will never change, chances are that community will not yet be available to you. It is all there in front of you, but you will only see what you already know or are ready to know. Sometimes, you may even be invited to join a community that aligns with your vision, but because of your cynic conversations, fears or disbeliefs, you say no to it. Remember, you can only see it if you are ready for it. So I say JUMP—go for it! Be willing to redesign yourself to bring yourself to the next level. Say yes to anything that sounds too good to be true! What do you have to lose? I believe the universe is always in perfect integrity and that it will provide everything we need when we let go and allow creation to flow through us.

I started the Gratitude Training in 2010, and since then, what has been generated is a community of leaders who are all committed to transform the world, a Source Movement. The Gratitude Community is a thriving community originated in South Florida with members across the United States and beyond. Its vision is to awaken the planet, maximize joy and actualize peace. Because of the commitment of this community, people's lives are transformed every day. We create abundance, joy and gratitude while standing for each other through trust, honesty and courage. I am still in awe over my creation and yet very clear that I did in fact manifest it all. Because of my commitment to my vision and to living by the five principles of the Source Movement, all I had to be was a space for creation to occur. That is all it takes. Once we shift our unaligned conversations, keep our promises, be responsible and in gratitude while being in service to the all, we begin to create peace around us and in the world. A supporting community is the environment, or the context, for it to manifest. Think of the community as the soil for your vision to manifest. In order to have the biggest possibility, get the best soil you can!

When I choose to be part of a community or create one, I make sure my principles are present in that community. If they are not, I either bring them or decide on a different community. You may ask, "If we create everything, why would we create a community that we would not want to be part of." I don't know. Why would we? You should have enough information by now to look. Maybe there is something there to learn, to see, to contribute. Look. Find your own answers.

So how do we hold community as a principle? We simply make it as important as any principle by which we choose to live. The second level of integrity we spoke of earlier is to have a set of principles we won't abandon. Find or create a community that values its principles, a community that will not sell out on what is important, a community that is willing to have you live by your principles without fail, a community that is a space for everyone to win, for everyone to thrive. We can hold community as a principle when we look at the importance of its presence for living a virtuous life and sharing our joy and gratitude as a whole, as one.

questions for
reflection

1) What communities am I a part of?

_____

_____

_____

2) Do they provide a fertile soil for my vision?

_____

_____

_____

3) What are the reasons I want to be part of a community?

_____

_____

_____

4) What are the reasons I do not want to be part of
   a community?

_____

_____

_____

5) Do I have fears that stop me from joining or starting a community? What are the fears?

_____

_____

_____

_____

6) What is a thriving community to me?

_____

_____

_____

7) What do I have to contribute to a community?

_____

_____

_____

call for
action

⮑ Create a community. Choose a vision or something that is important to you, and start your own community around it. This can be a book club, a Facebook group, a Meetup, a running club, or anything you want.

⮑ Join a community that is aligned with your vision, and contribute to that community. Rather than being a passive member, get involved and offer your services. See what you can generate when you come from a place of surrender and giving. Can you be the catalyst for having the community thrive?

chapter eleven

a call to action

Be the change you want to see in the world.
—Gandhi

wareness is the first step to any transformation. Without the awareness, we are asleep. Many people are becoming aware right now; they are awakening. Awareness is an integral part of Source Movement. However, without some action, not much will change. If we really want to make a difference and own that we are Source for everything in our reality, we get to take actions that will support transformation for everyone. What I am saying is this: Be the change you want to see in the world! Gandhi said it best. His quote summarizes this whole book. How do we "be" that? How do we "do" that? I say it is time to break through anything that stops us from living our full potential and on purpose, to let go of all the beliefs, stories and conversations that do

not serve us, surrender to our commitments instead of being a
victim to our circumstances, be responsible for everything in our
reality, own our power as creator of our reality, spread love and
gratitude in our relationships, families, and communities, and
live fully in integrity with Source's intention for us. Simply, just
_BE_ the change.

the gratitude training

My awareness and awakening to *being the change,* was a direct
result of attending transformational trainings, having direct
experiences of living by the principles of Source Movement, and
completing the three steps to a joyous and abundant life in gratitude, mentioned in Chapter 8.

After completing the leadership program I attended when I
bumped into Don Warms at the airport and finishing the Giving Year as a result of that encounter, I knew I held the magic
formula for love. I am using the word love here because it encom-
passes joy, gratitude, and peace. The formula was: Gratitude
Consciousness + Source Movement Principles = Love Concise-
ness. Love consciousness, the opposite of fear consciousness, is
a state of peace, gratitude and joy. It is a state of being and a
context where you experience abundance in all areas of your life,
and the result is peace on a larger scale, namely world peace.

I wanted to offer the fastest way to accomplish living from this
abundant context, which is why I founded the Gratitude Training, a three-part curriculum that will accomplish just that—in
four months!

I worked with some of the most experienced trainers and

facilitators of transformational work in the world, and together we designed a curriculum that would create nothing less then extraordinary results for individuals and the world at large. We combined ancient philosophical thought, the best of transformational technologies, and added the distinctions of Gratitude and Community, all within a context of abundance, unconditional love, and forgiveness.

In short, the Gratitude Training is founded on the principles of Source Movement and, in my experience, the fastest way to individual and worldwide awakening. The Gratitude Training is a catalyst for Source Movement on a global scale. It is my goal that as many people as possible take this training so that we can together be the change to transform this world from a mass consciousness of scarcity and fear to abundance and love. I believe we can reach a point when the Gratitude Training is no longer needed. When enough people step into being a contribution and living from the principles of Source Movement, our next generations will be born into the Gratitude Context and already Source for peace.

living by the principles

The principles of the Source Movement set you up to win. I have seen the results of personally living by them for many years now. We will know if we are living on purpose and according to our vision by looking at our results. Many times we don't like what we see when we do so, but my invitation is to own ALL your results and hold them as a direct link to where you are in your own awakening and in your personal Source Movement.

For instance, I still experience asthma sometimes when I'm around cats. My "new" belief or vision, after reading books and having an experience of no asthma for years in the past, is that my asthma can disappear just by changing the conversation I have about it. However, my result today still is that I sometimes experience asthma. All this tells me is that I still have some work to do. Not from a good or bad place, but simply from a place that my vision of "no asthma" can't be aligned with the conversation I have about it because if it were, I would see the result.

An interesting point here is this, a few years ago, I was studying A Course in Miracles with a group here in South Florida. They had a set of principles, a set of rules to live by, during the yearlong study. They had set these rules to create what they believed would be the best environment for awakening. One of the rules was that you could not take ANY medication of any form while studying with this group. At the time, I lived with my two cats and had to use my asthma inhaler on a regular basis, especially at night. I made a decision to join the group anyway and discarded all medications, including Advil. The first couple months were challenging, but I was committed to working this out. I was committed that I could overcome asthma simply by not being an environment for asthma (i.e., having inhalers, believing I had it, etc.). After about three months, all my symptoms of asthma were gone! For two years, I had no asthma! So now we may ask why I sometimes experience asthma again. I believe it is just a gauge of where I am with my principles and my own personal awakening. It does not matter how awake we are; we can all fall asleep in an instant, and we do every day. Rigor and practice is what keeps us living as our highest selves. I had that rigor during those two years, and the results showed it.

Let's explore the concept of principles as being a set of rules. Many of us cringe at the notion of "rules," as we have been conditioned by rules our whole life. I want you to open a space to see your principles and the principles of Source Movement as a set of rules by which to live—so much so that you are willing to give your word that you will live by them. Put yourself on the line. There is a level of trust required to surrender to rules and principles.

For instance, when I agreed to not take any medication for a year, my parrot was screaming at me, telling me it is impossible. However, I had a level of trust that I was ready for this challenge. If you don't have that level of trust, it may just be a reflection that you are not ready for what you are about to embark on. It may not be "right" for you at this time. Be careful here, though. That does not mean that what is in front of you is "wrong" or that you are "bad" for not being able to do something. It is a neutral event. There is no need to judge it as anything else. I did that at first. I made the study group "wrong" for putting the rule of no medication in place, and I judged and talked about it so my parrot could feel safe and that nothing was going to change. Once I realized that the rule was there to serve me, to have me break through a conversation that I had been having my whole life, I was able to embrace the challenge. I was ready. I want to reiterate here that I am in no way suggesting that you stop taking your medication. I am simply sharing a personal experience to illustrate a point.

The right set of principles, or rules to live by, set up an environment for you to be free. Isn't that funny? Most of us think that rules imprison us or have us be followers. I say, not the right rules. They create a context, a fertile ground for growth and breakthroughs. They make change certain and safe. Even though they may seem scary and unsafe at times. Once you teach your parrot the new set of rules and you begin to embody these principles in your life, you and your parrot will be free, and the fun begins!

Let me give you another example. In the Gratitude Training, you are asked to give your word to a set of ground rules. The rules are there to open up a bigger possibility for you and to create the best and safest environment for your discovery and breakthrough. One of the rules is simple: Be on time. Many of us can agree to be on time, and we do many times in our lives. However, when asked to give your word that you will be on time, the students usually end up in uproar. They exclaim, "What if there is traffic?" or "What if my car breaks down?" There are suddenly a million possible circumstances that would have them not give their word to be on time. *We are so afraid to break our word that we are not even willing to give it.* We would rather not agree to a principle or a rule because of the fear and belief that if we don't honor it we will look bad or fail. Fear of failure is why most people are afraid to make commitments. *We would rather be a person who does not make commitments than one who breaks them.* Here is the catch: If we don't make commitments, give our word and make promises, we close the space—the possibility for anything to occur. We close the door on success for all the things we want.

Making a decision to live by the principles of Source Movement can be quite an undertaking if you resist it. It can also be just that: a decision, simple and clear. You choose. Either way, the invitation is to join this movement with me—consciously. I say that because I believe we are all in this movement already; some are just not aware of it, and some may be aware but have not made the distinction by giving it a name. We are now. We call it Source Movement. When beginning or continuing to live by these principles, we will be challenged every day by our parrot that will fight to keep what it knows, but will eventually scream to be retrained. We will retrain it.

be the change

Earlier in this chapter, we quoted Gandhi, "Be the change you want to see in the world." How do we do that? This may look different for all of us. Find what it is for you. Are you afraid of being in an intimate relationship? If so, go out there and create that magic relationship. Be willing to lose it all; be willing to get your heart broken again and again, and then go for it again. This is what life is about—us standing courageous in the face of fear and going for it anyway. Maybe you have conversations about money that keep you broke or always reaching for more. If so, be willing to turn yourself inside out to let go of those stories that keep you stuck, get the support you need, read the right books, take a workshop, try new things, be willing to fall flat on your face and then get back up again, and reinvent yourself. If you have tried everything to lose weight and you feel like there is nothing else you can do, it's time to explore new ways of thinking and do something that will have you be outwardly focused. Be in service to someone else. Work on shifting your beliefs about yourself that have you stay stuck.

I don't know what it is for you. But I do know this: If you choose to live by the five principles of Source Movement, you are well on your way to a transformed life in joy and abundance. You just have to be willing to get committed and apply them fully in your life. If you do that authentically, you will see transformation. You will see a major shift in your family, your community, and ultimately in the world. You have nothing to lose. We have nothing to lose and everything to gain.

a token of my appreciation

Before we part ways, I have one request of you. There is a gift from me to you included with this book. With a TOFA token, I want to thank you for making a difference in my day and taking the time to read my book. It means the world to me. My request is that you register it online at TOFA.us and give it to someone in your life for making a difference in your day. Pay it forward. Be the change. Be Source Movement.

resources

Source Movement Website—*www.Source-Movement.com*
Gratitude Training Website—*www.GratitudeTraining.com*
TOFA Website—*www.TOFA.us*
Jo Englesson Website—*www.JoEnglesson.com*
Gratitude Products Website—*www.GratitudeProducts.com*

recommended readings

A New Earth by *Eckhart Tolle*
A Course In Miracles
Seven Spiritual Laws of Success by *Deepak Chopra*
Busting Loose from the Business Game by *Robert Scheinfeld*
Conversations with God (Book 1) by *Neale Donald Walsch*
The Four Agreements by *Don Miguel Ruiz*
Mastery of Love by *Don Miguel Ruiz*